The Symbolic Dimensions
of the American Presidency

Description and Analysis

The Symbolic Dimensions
of the American Presidency
Description and Analysis

Robert E. Denton, Jr.
Georgia Military College

Waveland Press, Inc.
Prospect Heights, Illinois

For information about this book, write or call:

Waveland Press, Inc.
P.O. Box 400
Prospect Heights, Illinois 60070
(312) 634-0081

Dedication

This book is dedicated to Robert, Alice, and Paula whose symbolic dimensions include father, mother, and wife.

Contents

Acknowledgments

A project, such as this book, clearly encompasses more than the countless hours of writing and research. To acknowledge the major influences and help received while pursuing this goal is difficult but indeed most enjoyable. I am greatly indebted to Professor Don Burks of Purdue University who, a number of years ago, instilled an appreciation for the principles of rhetorical theory and forever compelled me to define rhetorical phenomena with precision, profundity, and pride. I am grateful to Professor Richard Crable of Purdue University whose comments on the manuscript resulted in sharper vision, more skillful application, and a greater horizon of artifacts for investigation. I am thankful to Professor Myron Hale of Purdue University whose knowledge of Presidents and the Presidency is almost limitless. His comments and insights have profoundly influenced my thinking and, consequently, this book. Professor Ralph Webb of Purdue University provided guidance in understanding and applying the concepts of symbolic interaction. And to my former major professor, Charles J. Stewart, goes my sincere, heartfelt gratitude. He guided, for several years, my intellectual endeavors with care, compassion, and excellence. His door was always open; he was always willing to offer advice, counsel, or simply friendly conversation. My indebtedness to him abounds for the numerous hours he spent reading the manuscript drafts and the detailed comments he provided. Finally, I wish to acknowledge the fine efforts of my publisher, Neil Rowe. For his belief and assistance in the fruition of this project, I am most grateful. All of these men, individually and collectively, sincerely cared, shared, and gave far more than I can ever reciprocate. I can only hope that their efforts were not in vain.

There is, however, life beyond attempts of scholarship and academic writing. I am indebted to my wife Paula, who was always supportive of this project proclaiming its merit which simply stemmed from believing in me. Such support is often the difference between success and failure.

Please do not hold the above individuals guilty by association for the faults and shortcomings of this study. I alone must bear that responsibility. Yet, I above all others recognize that the true significnce and value of this work transcends its meager findings. Rather, its value lies in the process of its creation, the relationships formed, and the resulting interactions.

Preface

The institution of the American Presidency is in a state of crisis. After two hundred years of confidence and stability, the office is now the center of great controversy and debate. Because of recent excesses and abuses of Presidential power; many Americans question the integrity of the office and are becoming increasingly cynical about the viability of the institution. Within recent years, the office of the President has become the object of critical study by numerous political scientists, commentators, editorial writers, former presidents, as well as various presidential assistants. Consequently, there are many who advocate retribution against the institution of the Presidency. Although unanimous in recognizing a "crisis" of the Presidency; there is little agreement as to what the "crisis" specifically is, why and how the "crisis" developed, and how the American people can defuse the "crisis." Clearly what is needed is a better understanding of the nature of the Presidency. In order to do this successfully, one needs to appreciate the symbolic dimensions of the office.

The purpose of this study is to present a systematic, theoretical description of the Presidency from an interactionist viewpoint while at least attempting to provide an additional perspective or approach to the study of the American Presidency. In doing so, the approach offers alternative ways to view traditional political concepts as Presidential roles, models, power, and leadership. The study also recognizes the importance of the symbolic, mythic nature of the office. Finally, when contemporaries are challenging the viability of the office, the study provides a framework for assessing the current state of the Presidency and the potential effectiveness of the institution in the future.

Historically, much has been written about American Presidents. Very little, however, has been written about the American Presidency. This book is one modest attempt at bridging that gap. The focus of the study is on the various dimensions and levels of interaction involving the Presidency. The levels of interaction include: individuals of the general public, the general public or society, and specific office holders as they mold and shape their behavior to meet the public's expectations of Presidential behavior. The symbolic nature of the office emerges from the various interactions and may be characterized as: synthetic, believable, passive, vivid, simplified, and ambiguous. Generally, the President serves as priest, prophet, and king. The perspective of symbolic interaction best reveals the public's response to the institution and their effect upon its nature. Finally, the study suggests that the "crisis" of the Presidency lies within the realm of the symbolic. Specifically, the nature of the "crisis" is the gap between the symbolic, mythic, historical Presidential personal and the harsh "realities" and "demands" of today's world. The nation's mythic, symbolic expectations of the office are no longer apropos to meet the challenges of the twenty-first century. There are three major factors which have contributed significantly to the formation of the "crisis." First, previous administrations have left legacies of Presidential conduct and behavior which have been deified, contributing to the formation of legends, heroes, and expectations of spectacular behavior. Second, the role of the mass media has increased emphasis of image over substance. The media often aids in reinforcing the "myths" of Presidential persona as well as in the construction of such myths. Third, the world has changed drastically since World War II both politically and economically. The United States is vitally dependent upon other nations for oil, various imports, and economic stability. Hence, these factors have significantly contributed to widening the gap between largely symbolic expectations and Presidential performance. As the gap increases so does the disillusionment of many Americans and the impotence of the Presidency. The end result of the widening gap would be to make the Presidency pure symbol with no referent and no substance.

Chapter 1

Introduction

The institution of the American Presidency is in a state of crisis. After two hundred years of confidence and stability, the office is now the center of great controversy and debate.[1] For Americans, the crisis is real indeed.

> One must go to the great tragedies of a Shakespeare for parallels. Yet, in the contemporary scene, the play and its denouncement were played on the stage of the entire world. The aftermath provokes on a majestic scale a thoughtfulness and soul-searching. These have always been the earmarks of a tragedy's evaluation of action to the level of universal predicaments and hope. They mirror the despair and determination of humanity.[2]

During the 1960 and 1970 decades, the United States passed through a tremendous internal political crisis that drained the nation's energy, taxed its patience, and threatened its constitutional system. Good intentions, inflated promises, and a commitment for action failed to solve the problems of the 1960's and 1970's. "Under the banners of the New Frontier, the Great Society, The New American Revolution, and WIN, the Presidents pledged major innovations and social change. Each also generated, however, a grievously large gap between promise and performance."[3] As Barber notes, "if as it now appears, the public voted for activism in 1960, for peace in 1964, for tranquility in 1968, and for competence in 1972, then somehow our calculus has been defective."[4]

The institution of the American Presidency is a paradox.[5] The office always seems too strong or too weak. A President appears to have too much

1

power for the realization of "self rule" while lacking enough power to solve this nation's most critical problems. The American public wants a common man in the White House but expects uncommon leadership. The public demands that a President be above "politics" while forgetting that to be elected an individual must be, above all, a politician. By acting decisively, the President is labeled "dictatorial" and "unconstitutional." But by failing to act decisively he is called "passive" and "weak." Why has such a paradoxical institution survived for more than two hundred years and served the American public well in the process?

Part of the answer lies in the fact that the institution is largely undefined. The Constitution is alarmingly vague on the responsibilities, dimensions, and roles of the office. Perhaps the office has survived and functioned well primarily because of its fundamentally symbolic nature. It is literally "all things to all people." Cronin argues that one of the overriding functions of the President is "...to provide symbolic affirmation of the nation's basic values and aspirations."[6] Yet, because of recent excesses and abuses of Presidential power, many Americans question the integrity of the office and have become increasingly cynical about the viability of the institution. There are those in Congress, in the academic community, and in the public at large who advocate retribution against the institution of the Presidency. Perhaps what is needed, rather, is to understand better the nature of the Presidency. To do this successfully, one needs to appreciate the symbolic dimensions of the office. Therein lies the understanding of the paradoxes of the Presidency.

Within recent years, the office of President has become the object of critical study by numerous political scientists, commentators, editorial writers, former presidents, and various presidential assistants.[7] Although unanimous in recognizing a "crisis" of the Presidency; there is little agreement as to what the "crisis" specifically is, why and how the "crisis" developed, and how the American people can defuse the "crisis." The various descriptions, explanations, and prescriptions of the office and "crisis" appear to evolve from eight traditional approaches to the study of the modern Presidency. These approaches are most commonly referred to as constitutional-legalistic, institutional, pluralist or interest group, elitist, behavioral, decision making, systems, and policy process approaches. Historically, these eight approaches have boasted the ability to describe the "essence" of the office, the nature of its power, and its salvation as an institution. Obviously, it is beyond the scope of this work to detail each of the approaches. It is necessary, however, to identify briefly the major thrust of each approach and its shortcomings in relation to this study.

Presidential scholar Myron Hale argues that before research begins, "a scholar must decide which is the most meaningful approach, general framework, or perspective to study his 'object of affection'."[8] Each approach necessitates focusing on different aspects of the Presidency ultimately influencing or affecting the findings, results, or outcomes of the study. Some of the approaches are primarily explanatory while others are mainly descriptive or prescriptive. They all, however, provide unique insight into the nature of the Presidency.[9]

Constitutional-legalistic discussions of the Presidency rest on the legal foundations of the institution.[10] Careful analysis of the Constitution, Congressional statutes, and Supreme Court decisions provide the primary basis for investigation. The major issue of concern for such scholars is Presidential power and authority as revealed in our rather legalistic governmental structure. This approach is perhaps the most "narrow" of all the approaches. Therein lies its greatest limitation. As Hale observes, " a legal analysis is not a political analysis."[11] This approach simply ignores the dynamics of the office. It treats the institution as strictly "empirically" defined, ignoring the emotional, symbolic significance of the office. Questions of Presidential power are observable and consequently clearly "right or wrong," "good or bad." This study argues that the emotional, mythical, and symbolic dimensions of the office are more important than even the constitutional definition of the office. The Presidency "lives" and "grows" contrary to statutes but rather in accordance to societal needs and expectations.

The institutional approach primarily views the office from a structural orientation.[12] The continual growth, expansion, and development of the office comprises the key concerns of this perspective. The question of how the institution has grown to meet the needs of the citizenry has led to organizational and management concerns. The epitomy of this approach lies in the attempt to find the "best" and most "efficient" political structure. Organizational theory comprises the major emphasis of this orientation today. Again, however, this approach ignores many "political" dimensions of the office. There is a big difference between "efficiency" and "effectiveness." Efficiency does not automatically guarantee psychological or emotional satisfaction. The Presidency is more than a management office. To identify a problem, isolate the variables, and construct a solution is not the same as generating support, persuading a public of a law's necessity, and getting the legislation passed through Congress. Leadership, as a quality, differs from simple management. Because the office is "public," structure alone is of little concern when attempting to gauge the significance of the office to the public.

The pluralism or interest group approach to the Presidency focuses on the behavior of various groups in society that share common interest or issues.[13] The unit of analysis is the cross section of human activity.[14] This approach views political activity as representation of demands in society founded in social and economic concerns. Various groups of shared interest compete for power, influence, and access to government reigns of control. Political actions are evaluated in terms of their effects on specified groups. Thus, political outputs or decisions are really the results of "group behavior." At least this perspective recognizes more dynamics of the office. It recognizes the role of societal factors in influencing the office. The occupant of the office must reflect or at least acknowledge the concerns of various groups in society. Yet, as the literature defines the area, it tends to ignore the influence of elitists in controlling the very demands and issues of the "interest groups."

The question arises as to the significance of issues proclaimed. Are the problems announced truly reflective of the opinions of a large number of citizens? Group concensus can certainly be fabricated and manipulated. If the various appeals are abstract enough, we all belong to many groups. The important question is the intensity of affiliation. One can argue that sheep, as a group, seek comfort and safety in numbers, but the shepherd is the one who dictates the parameters of movement and limits of food. Societal laws can be potent independent variables in patterning human behavior. With the powerful but passive role of mass media, it has become rather easy to proclaim wide support. Public versus private interest is largely a matter of myth. Are Presidents to be viewed simply as "interest group leaders" with their sole task to function as bargainers of special interests? The office encompasses *all* Americans. Once elected, the President is indeed President of all the people for a set period of four years no matter the margin of electoral victory. In most inaugural addresses, a new President proclaims to speak for "all Americans whether democrat or republican; rich or poor; black or white."

The elitist approach emphatically states that a recognizable "ruling class" exists.[15] This "ruling class" is comprised of a self-conscious elite who controls society. The approach emphasizes clear human differentiation within organized groups. Within each human activity are those individuals who exercise domination over others. Elites comprise the major hierarchies and organizations of society. Consequently, the important decisions in our society are made by a "power elite." Elitist's power may be based upon wealth, education, or social status. Nevertheless, this approach lessens the impact of individual input and freedom. It argues that our government is maintained by a "circultion of elites." Presidents may "come and go" but the real decision-makers or power brokers simply "rotate" around in government and comprise a relatively small number of individuals. At least this approach, almost to an extreme, recognizes the role of a select few individuals "contriving," "maniuplating," and "leading" the masses. It almost assumes, in a rather strict sense, a unity of agreement among elites in terms of "what to do" and "how to do it." We know, of course, from experience that this is certainly not the case. (One need only investigate the continuous disagreement of "elite" economists about the regulation of our economy to prove the point). Specifically, in terms of the Presidency, no distinction is made between governing and nongoverning elites. We are too well aware of the fact that the "best" does not always win. Leaders are selected for a variety of reasons. There is, in our system above all others, a distinction too often forgotten between campaigning and governing; between leadership and management. In addition, with the continual increase of the role of media in Presidential politics a "nobody" can become a "somebody" and be elevated to the Presidency despite background or experience (i.e., George McGovern or Jimmy Carter). In this age, a "celebrity" is not the same as an "elite" in the traditional usage of the term.

Currently, the popular behavioral approach to the Presidency focuses on the individual occupant of the office.[16] The goal of such scholars is to identify the "ideal" or "best" models of personality types to be Presidents. Thus, models and categories of personality types are developed. From these models, criteria are established for evaluating and judging potential Presidents. The task of the public, therefore, is simply to find the "ideal" type to become President. This approach is founded on the belief that personality variables influence an individual's behavior, approach to the job, and decision-making capabilities. Although the literature in this area is most fascinating and entertaining, it simply suffers from reductionism by ignoring too many variables of influence. The perspective is dangerously interpretive and subjective; it fails to recognize the capabilities of an individual, at various times, to "move across" personality types. In addition, it may be argued, that at certain times our nation needed and responded to varied personality types. After World War II our nation needed the stability of an Eisenhower. After the barrage of social legislation of Lyndon Johnson we needed the restraint of Richard Nixon. Perhaps most importantly, the approach diminishes the role of institutional influence. Buchanan argues most effectively that there are common exposures, influences, or experiences all occupants of the Presidency must confront.[17] This study will certainly argue that the institution has a "life of its own." An individual must adapt to or adopt the public's historical expectations of the office and Presidential behavior. Finally, does the President confront a pre-established "reality" or is a President always compelled to create an acceptable "reality" for the public?

The decision-making approach to the office is also rather narrow.[18] Concrete proposals, actions, or decisions are a product of a decision-making process. Thus, to judge the value, correctness or quality of a decision, the scholar must focus on the decision-making process. This demands analyzing the organizational context, the accuracy of information, the motivations of participants, and the consequences of the decisions. Within this approach, crisis decision-making has received the most attention (i.e., Truman's decision to drop the Atomic bomb, Kennedy's Bay of Pigs and Cuban missile crisis, Johnson's Vietnam entanglement, Nixon's Watergate difficulties, Ford's *Mayaquez* mission, Carter's failed rescue attempt of American hostages in Iran, etc.). This approach attempts to explain, analyze, describe, and evaluate crucial decisions made by Presidents. Such analysis isolates and magnifies the importance of many variables in the decision-making process. The difficulty, of course, is that this approach lacks real objective criteria. Description is fine but in the realm of evaluation questions arise. There really is no way to make decisions with "full," "all," or "complete" information. In reality, this is a rather narrow, fragmented approach. It clearly fails to provide a broad perspective of what the Presidency entails as an office.

The systems and policy process approaches to the Presidency, in many ways, are the most encompassing of all the approaches.[19] The systems approach views political behavior as a system of behavior subject to many influences from the environment. "The political system is defined as that set of interactions relevant to the process of authoritatively allocating values for a society."[20] The political system is usually depicted as a means for resolving differences that are processed as "outpus." The "outputs," therefore, are results of the policy process. Microscopically, policy process scholars identify models of bargaining, conflict, and negotiation.

Interestingly, both approaches espouse to be empirical, constructively adaptive, and analytic in nature.[21] In terms of the Presidency, the office is viewed as only one element of our governmental system. However, as Hale observes, "very few scholars have used a vigorous and demanding systems approach when studying the institutionalized Presidency."[22] Nevertheless, this approach does recognize more variety of variables that affect the nature of the Presidency than most other approaches. Yet, the approach fails to assess critically the very nature of "inputs." System "inputs" are not simply a synthesis of societal beliefs, attitudes or values. Rather, they are subject to manipulation and control. In fact, it is often hard to distinguish between system "feedback" and system "inputs." Although providing a "wholistic" alternative to studying the Presidency, the systems approach lacks a clear framework for treating the office as a sub-system.

Does such an abundant number of critical approaches accurately identify, diagnose, and describe the "crisis" of the modern Presidency or even the office itself? In my opinion, they do not. Upon reviewing the relevant literature, one is favorably amused by E.E. Schattschneider's defining of political science as a mountain of data surrounding a vacuum.[23] Since the founding of the nation, Americans have nearly always favored solving problems by reforming structures. The above approaches all provide rather mechanistic explanations of the American Presidency. Increasingly, it is becoming clear that structures are only a small part of the Presidency. Structures, in fact, are arranged by individuals with unique perceptions, beliefs, and attitudes which play a significant role in the ultimate uses of those structures. In addition, they exist in a cultural context consisting of specific norms and expectations. Hence, the "crisis" of the modern Presidency and the nature of the office go beyond the constitutional-legalistic questions, the institutional organizational charts, the pressures of economic elites or interest groups, the specialized "inputs" and "outputs" of policy, and the "real" personality of individual Presidents.

Virtually every American, from seven to seventy, has a list of criteria of what makes a "good" President. Yet, when consulting the ultimate authority, Article II of the Constitution which delineates the functions and duties of the President, one notices how short, sketchy, vague, and almost trivial the description of the office appears. As Wilfred Brinkley observes, "...if the mythical man from Mars were to arrive and, by some miraculous means, were to become cognizant of every clause of the Constitution, every statutory provision and every judicial judgment pertaining to the President, he would yet be woefully ignorant of the Presidency as an institution."[24]

Although the Presidency is indeed a very real office with an elected official, space, desks, and staff; it remains elusive and undefined. "The Presidency is the work of the Presidents."[25] Expectations are created through Presidents' rhetoric, use of symbols, rituals, and sense of history. "Americans are taught at home, in the schools, and in pervasive political rhetoric that America is the land of equal opportunity; that there is equality before the law; that government accurately reflects the voice of the people, but does not shape it; that political and economic values are allocated fairly."[26] Within such an environment, as Rossiter notes, the President becomes "...the one-man distillation of the American people" reflecting their perceived dignity and majesty.[27] Consequently, elaborate criteria are envisioned for the man who desires the "sacred" office.

"...Candidates must try to conform to the public stereotypes of goodness, a standard which is typically far more demanding of politicians than of ordinary mortals."[28] By being "one of us," the President should naturally reflect the qualities comprising the "average American citizen" perpetuated in the myth of the "American character." "A candidate is helped by being thought of as trustworthy, reliable, mature, kind but firm, a devoted family man and in every way normal and presentable."[29] But these attributes alone are apparently not enough. Americans require a sense of direction and strength. As James Barber recognizes, "...children want to believe the President is a good man, that people turn to the President for a sense that things will be all right; that in the midst of trouble is a core of serenity, and that our ordinary ease will be sustained."[30] Herein lies the beginning of the paradox.

Purpose and Rationale

This is an institutional study and not a presentation of vignettes of specific Presidential actions and behavior. In fact, an abundance of the latter has created a lack of knowledge and appreciation for the institution. As James MacGregor Burns argues, "Thanks to reporters and historians we have had a superabundance of facts about American Presidents...No institution of American government suffers so much from what David Easton calls hyperfactualism. In a sense we know everything about the Presidents and nothing about the Presidency."[31] Perhaps this is true because, as Wilson noted, it is much easier to write about a President than to write about the Presidency.[32]

The Presidency, as an institution, does indeed respond to the laws of Darwin. The institution is ever evolving and changing. "No matter what the Constitution of 1787 prescribed for the office of President," according to Wilfred Brinkley, "deep-seated forces inherent in American society, playing upon the Presidency for more than two centuries have transformed the office created by the framers into the unique institution the Presidency is today."[33] Most often, the "scientists" of politics search for indisputable data, measurable elements, and clear decisions of the office. Yet, the Presidency defies simple analysis. The Presidency is a product of interaction. The institution is comprised of the public's historic, mythic perceptions and expectations of the office. It "grows" as individual occupants and situations mold, shape, create, and reinforce various public perceptions and expectations of the office. The Presidency *is not* what goes on behind closed doors. Its true significance and impact lies in its public domain. The American political system is not simply a historical structure. Rather, it is a composition of people and becomes a social object that is selectively conceptualized, interpreted, and reinforced resulting from the interaction of people within the structure.

The basic element of politics is talk. As Peter Hall observes, "On the one hand, politics consitutes the transformation of physical confrontations into verbal ones, and on the other, the resolution or accommodation of these confrontations involves the use of political rhetoric. ...We must be therefore interested in understanding the processes of political talk in determining how the audience is activated."[34] In terms of the Presidency, "perhaps all the sweep of Presidential leadership becomes more visible and sensible," according to Emmet Hughes, "when looked upon as a political mystery rather than a political institution."[35] Cronin agrees at least in part by noting:

> In any event, the informal and symbolic powers of the Presidency today account for as much as the formal ones....In some ways the modern Presidency has virtually unlimited authority for nearly anything its oc-

cupant chooses to do with it. In other ways, however, our beliefs and hopes about the Presidency very much shape the character and quality of the Presidential performances we get.[36]

Political sicentists, generally, have failed to examine the dynamic, internal processes of the political system, the impact of political outputs and "symbols" upon society, and the creation of "symbolic political reality" by agents of the system. The purpose of this study is to examine the institution of the Presidency of the United States from a symbolic interactionist perspective. In so doing, a greater understanding and appreciation for the dynamic, processual, and symbolic dimensions of the office results. Specifically, this study investigates three levels of interaction of the institution of the Presidency and the American citizenry. The levels of interaction include: individuals of the general public, the general public or society, and specific office holders. The following considerations evolve from investigating the three levels of interaction:

1. how public perceptions and expectations influence, mold, create, and restrict the Presidency as well as Presidential behavior,
2. how an individual adapts and adopts the historical, symbolic, and mythical qualities of the office, and
3. what the implications are of such an approach to the office upon society and Presidential job performance.

The following assumptions are important in formulating the study and in selecting the theoretical perspective of symbolic interaction.

1. The institution of the American Presidency is greater than any individual. The office greatly influences the office holder who must confront already established expectations of Presidential performance and behavior.
2. The set of expected Presidential roles result from the interaction of the office with the public. The role sets are created, sustained, and permeated through interaction comprised of campaigns, socialization, history, and myth.
3. The Presidency, as an institution, has several important consequences on public behavior that have been largely ignored by traditional approaches to the study of the office.

As mentioned earlier in this chapter, many Americans hold the office in less esteem due to recent excesses and abuses of Presidential power. Some advocate reprisals against the institution for such misuses. What clearly is needed is a better understanding of the nature of the Presidency. To do this successfully, one needs to appreciate the symbolic dimensions of the office.

The primary yield of this research study is to increase understanding of the Presidency. Second, the symbolic aspects of the office have largely been ignored by many scholars of Presidential politics. This study, therefore, is one of the first systematic investigations of the Presidency from a symbolic interactionist perspective. More specifically, the study recognizes the importance of the symbolic, mythic nature of the office. In addition, if the Presidency, as argued by several contemporary scholars, is in a state of "crisis" the perspective offered by this study more clearly exposes the fundamental nature of the "crisis" than have previous approaches. Most importantly, mechanical, institutional changes of the Presidency are of a "quick fix" nature. That is, institutional changes confront only the more obvious symptoms of problems rather than the causes of problems. The average citizen seldom appreciates or understands constitutional arguments for changing the structure of the office. Rather, the average citizen responds to a "Presidential" persona comprised of myth, image, goals, hopes, etc. Thus, any reform of the Presidency must begin with a consideration of the public's perceptions of the office and the accuracy of the perceptions in the world of "reality."

Methodological Considerations

Herbert Blumer, in 1937, coined the term "symbolic interactionism" to characterize the work of a rather diverse group of scholars including the pragmatic philosophers George Herbert Mead, William James, John Dewey, Charles Peirce, and the sociologists W.I. Thomas, Robert Park, Charles Cooley, and Louis Wirth.[37] Symbolic interactionism breaks away from traditional social science and views the human as maker, doer, actor, and self-director. The perspective focuses on socially created human qualities which counter "deterministic" traditional social science. In contrast to other perspectives in social psychology, symbolic interactionism focuses on the nature of interaction rather than on individual attitudes, personality, or social structure. The basic unit of analysis in any interactionist account is the joint act or the interactional episode. The symbolic interactionist seeks to understand the activities of interacting individuals.

Humans are conceptualized as influenced by their "perspectives" (perceptions) which are always dynamic, guiding influences. Humans do not passively respond to social stimuli but actively interpret and guide the social situation. Perspectives (perceptions) are learned through communication (or interaction) and the individual can take on one of many perspectives, each one associated with a reference group. A society, therefore, is conceptualized as individuals in interaction developing a common, shared perspective. The individual is not seen as shaped by society but as actively involved in its development.

Blumer states three major premises of symbolic interactionism:

1. Human beings act toward things on the basis of the meanings that the things have for them;
2. The meaning of things is derived from, or arise out of, the social interaction that one has with people; and
3. Meanings are handled in, and modified through, an interpretive process used by the person in dealing with the things he encounters.

From these premises three key concepts have evolved as the major "tools of analysis" for symbolic interactionists: self, society, and "mind" (i.e., knowledge). These concepts are important in that they are integral to the theory of symbolic interractionism and serve as the foundation for investigative efforts. Taken together, they allow for an explanation of relationships and thus better enable an understanding and explanation of human behavior.

Each of the concepts is vitally important in attempting to appreciate the nature of the Presidency. This study will analyze the Presidency utilizing the three theoretical concepts. Specifically, each level of interaction investigated in this study utilizes as a focal point one of the three concepts identified above. When viewing the interaction of the institution of the Presidency with individuals of the citizenry, the focus is on "mind" or the "nature" and "understanding" of the office that arises. This "understanding" comprises the public's definitions and expectations of the Presidency. When considering the interaction of the office with the office holder, the focus is on the evolving of a "Presidential self." This level of interaction encompasses the various steps involved as an individual adapts and adopts historical, symbolic, and mythical qualities of the office. The interaction of the institution of the Presidency with the general public concerns the impact or influence of the office on the fabric of society. This level of interaction recognizes the role of the office in relation to social control. Investigating these levels of interaction by utilizing the theoretical concepts of "mind, self, and society" reveals more accurately the perceptions the public has of the Presidency, its expectations of Presidential behavior, the societal function or role the Presidency plays in society, the symbolic requirements of the office, and when confronted, the nature of the current "crisis" of the modern Presidency.

This study is comprised of six chapters. Chapter Two explains further symbolic interactionism as an area of study and its application to the study of the American Presidency. Chapter Three focuses on Presidential roles; how Presidential roles are created, sustained, and permeated through society. Distinctions are made among Presidential functions, roles, and models. The process of an individual "becoming" President or adapting to the office is also observed. Chapter Four investigates the symbolic environment or "situation" of the American Presidency. Specifically, the chapter views how elements of the Presidential environment are created, arranged, manipulated, and controlled by individuals and the resulting implications upon societal behavior. Chapter Five identifies the major implications of a symbolic interactionist understanding of the office. Chapter Six speculates about the future of the Presidency and briefly suggests how the institution should be viewed in order to strengthen the office.

Footnotes

[1] Recent major works that have recognized an "institutional" crisis include: George Reedy, *The Twilight of the Presidency*; Joe McGinniss, *The Selling of the President 1968*; Arthur Schlesinger, *The Imperial Presidency*; Michael Novak, *Choosing Our King*; James D. Barber, *The Presidential Character*; Bruce Buchanan, *The Presidential Experience*; and Theodore White, *Breach of Faith*.

[2] Ernest S. Griffith, *The American Presidency* (New York: New York University Press, 1976), p. vi.

[3] Thomas E. Cronin, *The State of the Presidency* (Boston: Little, Brown, and Co., 1975), p. 4.

[4] James D. Barber, *Choosing the President* (New Jersey: Prentice-Hall, Inc., 1974), p. 2.

[5] For a good treatment of the paradoxical nature of the Presidency see Cronin, pp. 1-22.

[6] Cronin, p. 4.

[7] See Barber, *The Presidential Character,* (Englewood Cliffs: Prentice-Hall, Inc., 1972); Pious, *The American Presidency* (New York: Basic Books, 1979); Berstein and Woodward, *All the President's Men* (New York: Simon and Schuster, 1974); Schlesinger, *The Imperial Presidency* (Boston: Houghton Mifflin Co., 1973); and Schandler, *The Unmaking of a President: LBJ and Vietnam* (Princeton: Princeton University Press, 1977).

[8] Myron Hale, *The President and the Policy Process,* to be published, p. 23.

[9] Chapter 2 of Hale's forthcoming book on the Presidency provides the only synthesis of the various orientations to the office. This chapter plus Michael Weinstein, *Philosophy, Theory, and Method in Contemporary Political Thought* (Glenview: Scott, Foresman, and Co., 1971) served as the major source of descriptions provided in this discussion.

[10] Nearly all major works on the Presidency must, of course, acknowledge the constitutional, historical creation of the office. For an example of a study which totally bases its significance on this approach see Edward Corwin, *The President: Office and Powers* (New York: New York University Press, 1967).

[11] Hale, p. 25.

[12] For example, see Aaron Wildavsky, ed. *The Presidency* (Boston: Little, Brown, and Co., 1969).

[13] See David Truman, *The Governmental Process* (New York: Alfred A. Knopf, 1951); David Easton, *The Political System* (New York: Alfred Knopf, 1953); Arthur Bentley, *The Process of Government* (Cambridge: The Belknap Press, 1967);

William Connolly, *The Bias of Pluralism* (New York: Atherton Press, 1969).

[14]For a good discussion on pluralism see Weinstein, pp. 104-126.

[15]See Gaetano Mosca, *The Ruling Class* (New York: McGraw-Hill, 1939); C. Wright Mills, *The Power Elite* (New York: Oxford University Press, 1956); Harold Lasswell, *Politics: Who Get What, When, How* (Cleveland; The World Publishing Co., 1958); Renzo Sereno, *The Rulers* (New York:Frederick Praeger, 1962); Peter Bachrach, *The Theory of Democratic Elitism* (Bostom: Little, Brown, and Co., 1967).

[16]See Harold Lasswell, *Psychopathology and Politics* (Chicago: University of Chicago Press, 1930); Edwin Hargrove, *Presidential Leadership; Personality and Political Style* (New York: MacMillan, 1966); James Barber, *The Presidential Character* (Englewood Cliffs: Prentice-Hall, 1972).

[17]Bruce Buchanan, *The Presidential Experience* (Englewood Cliffs: Prentice Hall, 1978).

[18]See Harold Lasswell, *The Decision Process* (College Park: University of Maryland, 1956); Richard Snyder, ed., *Foreign Policy Decision-Making* (New York: Free Press, 1962); David Braybrooke and Charles Linbloom, *A Strategy of Decision* (New York: Free Press, 1963); Graham Allison, *Essence of Decision: Explaining the Cuban Missile Crisis* (Boston: Little, Brown, and Co., 1971).

[19]See Gabriel Almond and Sidney Verba, *The Civic Culture* (Princeton: Princeton University Press, 1963); David Easton, *A Systems Analysis of Political Life* (New York: John Wiley and Sons, 1965); H. Wiseman, *Political Systems* (New York: Frederick Praeger, 1967); Morton Kaplan, *Macropolitics* (Chicago: Aldine Publishing, 1969).

[20]Weinstein, p. 197.

[21]Weinstein, p. 205.

[22]Hale, p. 42.

[23]As reported in Barber, *Choosing the President,* p. 6.

[24]Wilfred Brinkley, *The Man in the White House: His Powers and Duties* (Baltimore: The John Hopkins Press, 1958), p. 1.

[25]Grant McConnell, *The Modern Presidency* (New York: St. Martin's Press, 1976), p. 9.

[26]Murray Edelman, *Politics as Symbolic Action* (Chicago: Markham Publishing Co., 1971), p. 55.

[27]Clinton Rossiter, *The American Presidency* (New York: Mentor Books, 1962), p. 16.

[28]Nelson, W. Polsby and Aaron B. Wildavsky, *Presidential Elections* (New York: Charles Scribner's & Sons, 1971), p. 190.

[29]Polsby and Wildavsky, p. 190.

[30]James D. Barber, "Man, Mood, and the Presidency" in *The Presidency Reappraised,* ed. Tugwell and Cronin (New York: Praeger Publishers, 1974), p. 206.

[31]James McGregor Burns, *Presidential Government: The Crucible of Leadership* (Boston: Houghton Mifflin Co., 1965), p. xii.

[32]As reported in Cronin, p. 5.

[33]Brinkley, p. i.

[34]Peter Hall, "A Symbolic Interactionist Analysis of Politics," *Sociological Inquiry,* 42, 1972 (3-4), p. 51.

[35]Emmet Hughes, *The Living Presidency* (New York: Penguin Books, 1973), p. 56.

[36]Cronin, p. 70.

[37]Herbert Blumer, *Symbolic Interactionism: Perspective and Method,* (Englewood
   Cliffs: Prentice-Hall, 1969), p. 6.

Chapter 2

Symbolic Interactionism: Perspective and Method

Introduction

A great many academic endeavors are overt attempts to understand the nature and social behavior of man. This is true because people are forced to live in relationships with others. Assessments of human relationships, however, do not occur within a vacuum. Individuals approach social phenomena from rather distinct perspectives. Perspectives or conceptual frameworks are "...really interrelated sets of words used to order physical reality. The words we use cause us to make assumptions and value judgments about what we are seeing (and not seeing)."[1] Formal education is a process of introducing one to a variety of perspectives; each of which presents a unique approach to "reality." Sociology, psychology, history, science, philosophy, to name a few, represent perspectives that individuals may adopt to guide their perceptions and interpretations of "reality." Of course, no perspective can account for "everything" and hence we are often limited by our perspectives.

The question should not become whether or not a perspective is true or false. More importantly, the question should be whether or not the perspective is useful in understanding social phenomena.[2] A useful perspective is one that allows for accurate description of what is occurring in the world. Therefore, "a good perspective gives us insight, clearly describes reality, helps us find the truths."[3]

Of all the perspectives in social science, perhaps the most controversial

15

and difficult to define is the area of social psychology. Some scholars would argue that social psychology is not a complete discipline or perspective, but merely a conglomeration of various topics and studies. Others, however, would argue that social psychology is indeed a discipline with its roots in both psychology and sociology and consisting of a unique history and subject matter.

Social psychology grew out of gestalt psychology in the late 19th and early 20th centuries.[4] The emphasis of gestalt psychology is on the nature of perception in human behavior. Attitude change is probably the most researched topic in social psychology. Other areas include: conformity, obedience, power, leadership, and attraction. More recently, social psychologists have investigated interpersonal communication, group decision making, and propaganda. Today, there are three major theoretical orientations in social psychology: balance theory, exchange theory, and symbolic interactionist theory.[5] Although the oldest of these three approaches, symbolic interactionism remains the least systematically developed theoretical orientation. Festinger has contributed a great deal to balance theory and Homas, Thibaut, and Kelly have contributed to the development of exchange theory.

But more important than topic areas is the "approach" of social psychology. The general concern is the analysis of the flow of individual experience. The emphasis is on "the subjectivity of the human actor," the "time-bound processes" of human behavior, and the "denial of external structure."[6] Social psychologists attempt to capture the flow of our own experience just as it is and to demonstrate that all else is a myth built up from individual performances.[7] Encompassing the rather broad concern of "the flow of individual experience" are several types of analysis: symbolic interactionism, social phenomenology, ethnomethodlogy, and sociological existentialism. For purposes of this study, symbolic interactionism is especially useful.

Symbolic interaction concepts provide a rather clear framework for investigating human communication behavior. The perspective highlights the signficance and importance of communication in determining human behavior by integrating traditional behavioral as well as humanistic approaches to the study of communication. To focus on social behavior requires an acknowledgement of the symbolic forces that are operative in society. Although descriptive in nature, when combined with communication orientations, symbolic interactionism can reveal guidelines for enhancing behavior between people. Hence, symbolic interactionism, in a broad context, is a communication theory of human behavior. In this chapter, symbolic interactionism will be defined; its historical origins and philosophical groundings identified; its major premises or assumptions recognized; and the major theoretical concepts discussed.

Definition

As a theory, symbolic interactionism is simply a specific way to make sense out of the world. If accepted, however, one is led to behave in certain ways and, consequently, to analyze the behavior of others and events in specified ways. "The term 'symbolic interaction,' refers to the peculiar and distinctive character of interaction as it takes place between human beings. The peculiarity consists in the fact that human beings interpret or 'define' each other's actions instead of merely reacting to each other's action."[8] Symbolic interactionism, therefore, focuses on the nature of interaction which comprises the dynamic social activities taking place between persons. As a kind of an analysis, it involves interpretation and definition.[9] The process of interpretation involves the ascertaining of meaning of various actions and remarks of others. The process of definition results in the sharing of how one is to act in a social context. These two processes result in participants fitting "their own acts to the ongoing acts of one another and guide others in doing so."[10].

The fundamental question for symbolic interactionists is, "How are people able to act together?" This question assumes that individuals live in both a symbolic and a physical environment. Consequently, it is because people can learn and use symbols that they are able to interact with others. Thus, the symbolic interactionist focuses on the interaction among individuals. The basic unit of analysis is the interactional episode. In attempting to understand the activities of interacting individuals, the behavior of any actor is conceived as a consequence of past interactional episodes. The "process" and "emergent" features of interaction, therefore, are stressed.

Perhaps the greatest controversy surrounding symbolic interactionism is its methodological application. Its methodological stance is the direct examination of the empirical social world. For symbolic interactionists, the empirical world is the natural world of group life. Hence, "it lodges its problems in this natural world, conducts its studies in it, and derives its interpretations from such naturalistic studies."[11] In order to study social movements, for example, the researcher should carefully trace the career, history, and life experiences of a movement. To study a religious cult, the researcher must go to the actual cult and observe member behavior through interaction.

Obviously, symbolic interactionism is a different, perhaps even radical approach from traditional empirical research approaches. It demands that scientific practitioners gain firsthand knowledge about the empirical world before formulating isolated theories about the world. Symbolic interactionism prefers "direct examination of actual human group life" to a contrived laboratory setting, scheme of operationalizing concepts, testing hypotheses, or force fitting of various premises to specified research procedure.[12] Thus, the value and validity of the concepts and propositions of symbolic interactionism are derived from direct examination of the world rather than from a view of the concepts after being subjected to "the alien criteria of an irrelevant methodology."[13] As Blumer succinctly argues:

> Symbolic interaction is not misled by the mythical belief that to be scientific it is necessary to shape one's study to fit a pre-established protocol of empirical inquiry, such as adopting the working procedure of advanced physical science, or devising in advance a fixed logical or mathematical model, or forcing the study into the mold of laboratory experimentation, or imposing a statistical or mathematical framework on the study, or organizing it in terms of preset variables, or restricting it to a particular standardized procedure such as survey research. Symbolic interaction recognizes that the genuine mark of an empirical science is to respect the nature of its empirical world — to fit its problems, its guiding conceptions, its procedures of inquiry, its techniques of study, its concepts, and its theories to that world.[14]

Historical Origins

The origins of symbolic interactionism are usually traced to the work of George Herbert Mead. As a professor of philosophy at the University of Chicago, Mead never systematically published his insights. Interestingly, it is a result of his students publishing Mead's lectures and their subsequent interpretation by various sociologists that have secured his influence. In fact, one of Mead's most notable students, Herbert Blumer, coined the term "symbolic interaction" in 1937 to characterize the work of not only Mead, but also of the pragmatic philosophers William James, John Dewey, Charles Peirce and sociologists W.T. Thomas, Robert Part, Charles Cooley, and Louis Wirth.[15] Others who have since made contributions to the perspective by showing theoretical and empirical applications include: M.H. Kuhn, Arnold Rose, Norman Denzin, Gregory Stone, Alfred Lindesmith, Anselm Strauss, Jerome Manis, Bernard Meltzer, and Tamotsu Shibutani.[16]

It is also important to recognize the influence of symbolic interactionism on other theoretical perspectives. Specifically, symbolic interactionism has significantly influenced labeling theory in the study of deviance, Erving Goffman's dramaturgical perspective, Garfinkel's ethnomethodology, and Kenneth Burke's dramatism.[17] Today, the influence of symbolic interactionism on mainstream sociological theory is most noticeable (see Figure 1).

Philosophical Grounding

There were three major philosophical influences on the thinking and teaching of George Herbert Mead which have greatly influenced the development of symbolic interaction theory. The first major influence was the philosophy of pragmatism. Mead substantially contributed to the develop-

Figure 1. Historical Origins of Symbolic Interaction

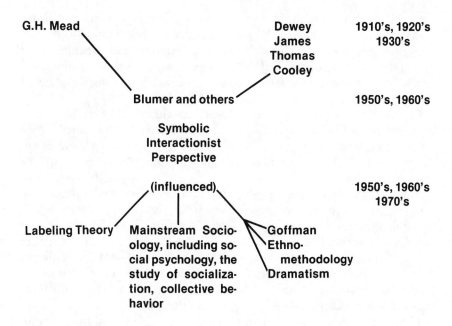

ment of this school of philosophy. This orientation offered a radical approach to the study of knowledge and truth. For Mead, all tests of knowledge ultimately involve subjective experience, perception, and interpretation. He faulted scientists' failure to question the existence of the world.[18] Science assumes the existence of the world which takes priority over subjective experience. Pragmatists had a major concern for bringing philosophical analysis to bear upon daily social issues. Finally, pragmatism had a great influence on Mead's approach to truth containing four basic principles:[19]

1. Truth is possible for the human being only through the individual's own intervention,
2. Knowledge for the human being is based on its usefulness,
3. Objects we encounter are defined according to their use for us, and
4. Understanding about the human being must be inferred from what one does.

One major assumption of the pragmatists, therefore, is that humans live in a world of meanings. One's response to events and objects are based on meanings attributed to them. Obviously, the meanings of events are not static and inflexible.

As the second major influence upon George Herbert Mead and hence symbolic interaction theory, Darwinism emphasizes that human beings are truly emergent in nature. Our universe is evolutionary and dynamic rather than static. Because of this belief, Mead argued that everything about the human being should be considered as "process" in a constant state of change rather than as stable or fixed.

The final major philosophical influence on George Herbert Mead was behaviorism. Meaning and consciousness of meaning were conceived to emerge from behavior. Behavior is not merely a "reaction" to stimulus but an "action" which may modify or create "meaning." This point will be emphasized later.

Although the influences of pragmatism, Darwinism, and behaviorism have contributed to the formation of a unified theoretical perspective, two major approaches or schools of symbolic interactionism have developed.[20] Herbert Blumer and his students developed what is called the "Chicago School" of interactionism which continues the classical Meadian tradition. The "Iowa School" of interactionism constitutes a major variant of the Median tradition based on the "self-theory" of Kuhn. There are three major differences between the two schools of thought.

The most fundamental difference between the Chicago and Iowa schools of interactionism is methodology. It is the classic difference between the humanistic and the scientific viewpoints. Blumer argues for a distinctive methodology while Kuhn argues that classical scientific methods should be utilized. For Blumer, the researcher "...must get inside the actor's world and must see the world as the actor sees it, for the actor's behavior takes place on the basis of his own particular meanings."[21] Thus, Blumer's research techniques include: participant observation, histories, autobiographies, case studies, diaries, letters, and interviews (nondirective types). In contrast, the Iowa school of interactionism stresses that the key ideas of symbolic interactionism can be operationalized in strict empirical research. In short, Kuhn sought to "empiricize" Mead's ideas by "reconceptualizing" them.[22]

The second issue of difference between the two schools revolves around the question of the degree to which man's behavior is free or determined. Blumer views human beings as active agents in creating their social environment. Individual behavior, therefore, is unpredictable and indeterminate. The Iowa school views the human being as relatively passive based upon the notions of positivism. Humans are mainly "internalizers" of stimuli which dictates behavior. Thus, behavior is determined by examination of conventional role theory and human conduct is predictable on the basis of internalized expectations.

Finally, there appears to be a process-structure distinction between the schools of interactionism. The "Chicago School" views self and society in "processual terms." In accordance with more traditional psychology and sociology notions, the "Iowa School" views self and society in more preconceived, structural terms. In sum, "while Blumer's image of man dictates his methodology, Kuhn's methodology dictates his image of man."[23] Despite these differences, however, there has grown a rather distinct body of concepts and ideas that constitute a theory of symbolic interaction. But before dealing in depth with specific concepts, it may be useful to recognize briefly some of the major assumptions and premises of symbolic interaction.

Major Premises and Assumptions

The nature of interaction is one of the major pillars of the theory of symbolic interactionism. Interaction is not so much a concept as an orientation for viewing man's behavior and, ultimately, society. People are constantly undergoing change in interaction and, consequently, society is also constantly changing through interaction. Interaction, as a process, involves acting, perceiving, interpreting, and acting again. This interaction among people gives rise to reality which is largely symbolic. Hence, it is through symbolic interaction with others that "meaning" is given to the world and create the reality toward which persons act.

But the importance of interaction is not only reserved for spoken and written language. Objects, of course, may exist in physical form. Such objects, however, for the human being are pointed out, isolated, catalogued, interpreted, and given meaning through social interaction. Hence, artifacts and objects are to be viewed as social objects. For the peasant, a rake is a gardening tool as well as a weapon for revolution. Such a transformation results from social interaction. Objects take on meaning for individuals as they interact with others.

It is also very important not to limit the importance of interaction to self-development. Interaction *is* the very fabric of society. Human society is most usefully conceived as consisting of people in interaction. "When two people interact, each influences the behavior of the other, and each directs one's own behavior on the basis of the other's behavior towards oneself."[24] Hence, for symbolic interactinists, behavior is *created* by interaction rather than occurring during interaction. For this reason, classical psychological qualities of an individual are of limited use in predicting behavior. "For behavior is a function of the interaction itself and not merely of those qualities which individuals bring into the interaction."[25] Interaction, therefore, is important for an individual's well-being as well as for the maintenance of the individual's beliefs, attitudes, and values.

Individuals interact within larger networks of other individuals and groups. Although many of society's networks are "far removed" from individuals, the impact of such networks may be considerable. Social networks, formal or informal, provide a framework within which social action takes place. Hence, the networks are not determinants of action. Even structural aspects of society, such as social roles, social class, etc., should be viewed as setting conditions for behavior and interaction rather than as causing specific behavior or interaction.

From this brief discussion, the significance of interaction for the symbolic interactionist should be evident. Interactionism dictates a rather clear approach or orientation to traditional concepts and variables of sociology as well as psychology. In sum,

> What a human being *is* depends upon interaction with others. And what a human being *does* depends not simply upon what kind of person he or she is (personality), but upon the person's interaction with others. At the same time, the individual is part of the interaction, acting and not merely reacting, creating and not merely being formed or controlled.[26]

Thus, "self" arises in interaction; symbols and language are defined in interaction; world views or perspectives arise in interaction and social objects are defined in interaction.

As reflected in the name of this perspective, the symbolic nature of man is also of prime importance. Distinctively human behavior and interaction are carried on through the medium of symbols and their attached meanings. The human being is a symbolic creature. Despite recent research with primates, sympathy exists for the view that what distinguishes humans from lower animals is their ability to function in a symbolic environment. Man alone can create, manipulate and use symbols to control his own behavior as well as the behavior of others. All animals, therefore, communicate. However, only human beings communicate with symbols.

What are symbols? To answer this question, according to Blumer, one must have an appreciation for "objects."[27] "An object is anything that can be indicated, anything that is pointed to or referred to."[28] There are three general categories of objects: physical, social, and abstract. Physical objects refer to "concrete" objects such as chairs, trees, desks, cars, etc. Social objects are generally people or positions occupied by people. This category includes students, a mother, priests, President, etc. Finally, abstract objects are moral principles, ideas or philosophical doctrines such as justice, love, freedom, etc. Each of these categories of objects has a symbolic dimension or may become a symbol. What an object "is" depends upon the "meaning" it has for an individual. The "meaning" will dictate how the individual sees the object, acts toward the object, and talks about the object. The President of the United States as an office or as an individual, will be addressed differently depending upon whether he is a member of the opposition party or an incumbent. Likewise, a President who fails to act decisively in a time of crisis may become a different object to the citizens. Common objects result from a process of mutual indications or being seen in the same manner by a given set of people. "In short, from the standpoint of symbolic interactionism, human group life is a process in which objects are being created, affirmed, transformed, and cast aside. The life and action of people necessarily change in line with the changes taking place in their world of objects."[29]

Mead defined symbols in terms of meaning. A system of symbols "is the means whereby individuals can indicate to one another what their responses to objects will be, and hence what the meanings of objects are."[30] The human, as a cognitive creature, functions in a context of shared meanings which are communicated through language (which is itself a group of shared meanings or symbols). Symbols, therefore, are more than a part of a language system. For Charon, "A symbol is any object, mode of conduct, or word toward which we act as if it were something else. Whatever the symbol stands for constitutes its meaning."[31] This definition, by Charon, has important implications for individual action as well as for the nature of society.

Nearly all human action is symbolic. Human action usually represents something more than what is immediately perceived. Symbols form the very basis of our overt behavior. Human action is the by-product of the stimulus of symbols. Before a response to any situation can be formulated, the situation must be defined and interpreted to ensure an appropriate response to the situation. Without exaggerating, therefore, symbols are the foundation of social life as well as of human civilization. Meanings for symbols derive from interaction in rather specific social contexts. New interaction experiences may result in "new" symbols or "new" meanings for "old" symbols which may, consequently, change one's understanding of the world. One's view of the world may change as that person's symbol system is modified through interaction. This notion suggests that one's social reality is made up of symbolic systems.

For the symbolic interactionist, reality is a social product arising from interaction or communication. Reality for everyone is therefore limited, specific, and circumscribed. Of course, communication can be used to extend or limit "realities." "In order to discover one's reality or the reality of another, it is necessary to understand the symbol system and what those symbols mean to the person using them."[32] Such mutual understanding is accomplished through communication.

Faules and Alexander argue that "reality" for individuals has three dimensions: "the outside world (i.e., knowledge) an inner private world, and a shared symbolic world of beliefs, experiences, and meanings generated and maintained through communication."[33] Reality, then, results from the sharing of experiences with others through symbol systems. Most importantly, the construction of reality is indeed an active process. It involves recognition, isolation, definition, interpretation, action, and validation through interaction. Communication becomes the vehicle for the creation of society, culture, rules, regulations, behavior, etc. From such a "chain of actions" grows a complex and constantly changing matrix of rather specific and varied individual as well as societal "expectations."

To have the capacity to learn culture (or the process of socialization) enables human beings to understand one another but at the same time creates behavioral expectations for one another which, finally, requires us constantly to orient our own behavior to that of others. The implications of this are important. It clearly stipulates a unique approach to social phenomena. For example, Klapp argues from this perspective that an individual is most successful in becoming a symbol by seizing cues offered by the public and then moving in the direction indicated.[34]

Hopefully, one now understands the interrelationship among symbols, interaction, and the nature of "reality." While not elevated to the level of individual "concepts," taken as a group they provide a distinct way to analyze and understand the human being. They function as "lens" through which to view human phenomena.

Before discussing key concepts of symbolic interactionism, it may be useful to state several premises of the perspective which may also serve as a brief review and synthesis. For Peter Hall, there are three major assumptions of symbolic interactionism.[35] First, "emergence" best characterizes the nature of human beings. The capacity of speech, language, thought, communication, and complex coordination of behavior distinguishes us from other animals. Because of such attributes, humans have fewer constraints than other animals and, hence, can create a world separate from the "exigencies of nature." Second, all aspects of human behavior must be viewed as in a state of "process." Man and society are dynamic and continuously in flux. Third, the emphasis of symbolic interactionism is on "action" and not structure. Man is defined as an actor rather than a reactor and as active rather than passive. Therefore, the human is the "creator" of the world in which he finds himself.

Herbert Blumer, in his classic *Symbolic Interactionism: Perspective and Method,* succinctly begins his book with "three simple premises" of symbolic interaction. The first premise states that "human beings act toward things on the basis of the meanings that the things have for them."[36] This premise recognizes the importance of meaning for human behavior. In typical psychological and sociological literature, meaning is reduced to finding "initiating or causative" factors or is viewed as a mere "transmission link' to behavior. Symbolic interactionists maintain that meanings of objects are important in their own right. The second premise states that "the meaning of such things is derived from, or arises out of, the social interaction that one has with one's fellows."[37] This premise refers to the source of meaning. As already noted, self, meaning, and behavior are products of interaction. Hence, the nature of any society truly depends on the nature of that society's interaction. Blumer's final premise deals with the individual's process of interpretation. "Meanings are handled in, and modified through, an interpetative process used by the person in dealing with the things he encounters."[38] Any actor must indicate to himself the things toward which he desires to act. Internalization and interpretation affects meaning which ultimately influences behavior or action.

As is true with all sciences, the researcher requires tools for proper investigation. For the social psychologist, "concepts" function as the fundamental tool of analysis. A concept, as defined by Lauer and Handel, is "an abstraction—a term or symbol that represents the similarities in otherwise diverse phenomena."[39] To clarify even more the perspective of symbolic interactionism plus how the perspective will be utilized in this study, the key concepts of mind, self, and society must be discussed. Each of these rather broad concepts has specialized terms or components which contribute to a more thorough understanding of the perspective. These concepts, although treated separately, are critically interrelated. Thus, the concepts are treated separately here to aid in better understanding their uniqueness. After a discussion of these concepts, an assessment of symbolic interaction as a method of study will be rendered.

"Mind and Self"

The human being is in a constant activity of self-indication or making notations of the various objects that one encounters. The human being, then, is an organism which confronts its world with a "mechanism" for making indications to himself. For the symbolic interactionist, the "mechanism" is a product of "self," "role," and interaction. The "self" is a social object that one shares with others in interaction. As noted already, an individual comes to "know" self in interaction with others. One's self is isolated, interpreted, and defined socially. The self becomes a separate object to an individual resulting from interaction with others. As an object, therefore, self can be modified, evaluated, and reinforced. To omit the "self" from interaction is to engage in a form of determinism. The notion of self-interaction emphasizes the dynamic nature of self and the importance of communication. William James stated that "a man has as many social selves as there are individuals who recognize him and carry an image of him in their minds."[40] The first point to be made is that the self is realized through interdependence with others.

Mead argued that the self emerges in three separate, sequential phases.[41] He called the phases "play," "game," and "the generalized other." As a child progressively goes from one stage to another, the child is better able to differentiate self from others. However, in the "game" phase, multiple roles are identified but not combined into a consistent symbolic perspective. It is in the last phase, "the generalized other," that an individual actively interprets one's experiences with others. Here the individual is capable of separating himself from the outside community. One is able to see self clearly in terms of the moral and symbolic expressions of others. Thus, "it is necessary to rational conduct that the individual should thus take an objective, impersonal attitude toward himself, that he should become an object to himself."[42] The act of "communication," then, provides a form of behavior in which a person is able to become an object to oneself. For Mead, "what is essential to communication is that the symbol should arouse in one's self what it arouses in the other individual."[43] This ensures a proper "response" or "action" in any situation.

From this discussion, four characteristics of self may be identified.[44] First, the self is a process and not merely some entity. As a process, behavior includes: "carving out a line of action that mediates between one's impulses and the expectations of the social environment; observing and responding to one's own and other's behavior; adjusting and directing one's subsequent behavior on these two bases."[45] Second, the self is reflexive. One may define, modify, and evaluate one's own behavior. Third, the self involves various attitudes which dictate behavioral expectations as well as proper responses to situations. Finally, related to the previous notion, the self is the primary means of social control. "To have a self is to internalize the attitudes of the community and thereby to control one's own behavior in terms of those attitudes."[46] Hence, social control is self-control.

I have, so far, emphasized how self is defined and evaluated to ensure "proper responses." Now, the task is to analyze the nature of "proper responses" which really discusses the nature of "mind." Symbolic interactionists have a term that describes how people organize their behavior. This term, of course, is "role." "Humans act toward one another on the basis of meaning acquired through social interaction. Out of this social interaction evolves a structure or model for behavior."[47] People define social situations by organizing perceptions of the situations into the roles played by others. In many ways, a role is simply the behavior of an individual which is accepted by others as an occupant of a given position, situation, or office.

Most often, roles exist prior to individuals. The social expectations of a role, therefore, may transcend individual actors. To make a point, although overstated, one might argue that it makes no difference who is President of the United States because the role possesses unique demands and behaviors independent of the specific person involved. In addition, because most roles demand certain qualities, people are forced to match "self" qualities with the demands of a particular role. Communication, of course, is important in executing a role. For example, many Americans believed that although President Ford was trustworthy, he was not strong and "tough" as a President should be in foreign affairs. However, when an American ship was seized, President Ford sent in the Marines to recover the ship as well as the crew. His action communicated a role expectation of strength and resolve of a President. Consequently, Ford's popularity in the national polls shot up. This phenomena is really quite common. Interestingly, although the Bay of Pigs as an invasion failed, Kennedy's popularity soared in the polls. In the Iranian "crisis," President Carter had to justify that "no action" was indeed proper action reflecting strength, resolve, firmness, fairness, etc.

Roles, then, are one aspect of behavioral patterns that help create societal expectations. Roles are defined socially and maintained through interaction or communication. An individual, therefore, must continuously engage in communication with "self" as one enacts the roles expected. An individual must constantly attempt to figure out what one's role in a situation is or should be. For a role presentation to be appropriate, therefore, not only must others perceive the behavior as proper but also individual self perceptions should be congruent with the role requirements.

One must not, however, think of a role as merely a "neat package of behavior" with a complete set of rules. Rather, the symbolic interactionist recognizes the reciprocal, interrelationships among roles. People constantly adjust behavior based on the reactions of others. Role behavior is negotiable. Human beings define a situation and behave according to predictions of another person's behavior. Thus, for each role there is a counter-role that one must understand in order to meet other people's role expectations.

The degree of personal freedom of behavior in any role enactment remains controversial. Perhaps as the self emerges through the different stages identified by Mead, the more formalized roles become. Even Blumer acknowledges that "the roles the person takes range from that of discrete individuals (the 'play stage'), through that of discrete organized groups (the 'game stage') to that of the abstract community (the 'generalized other')."[48] Social structures in society may provide rather clearly defined modes of behavior. Many offices, such as the Queen of England or President of the United States, may have the various behaviors, powers, duties, etc., carefully formulated or even written into various documents (i.e., charters, constitutions, etc.). Gerth and Mills argue that recognized institutions are "organizations of roles" which carry different degrees of authority.[49] As such, roles aid in maintaining social stability by facilitating guidelines and predictability in human interaction. At the very least, social positions provide guidelines for behavior.

Part of the process of selecting the proper role as well as fulfilling the expectations of a role is the notion of "roletaking." Roletaking is important in the development of self. It is the ability to roletake that allows one to see self through others. Roletaking enables a person to see the world from another's perspective and to direct his/her behavior accordingly. Roletaking is defined by Lauer and Handel as "the process whereby an individual imaginatively constructs the attitudes of the other, and thus anticipates the behavior of the other."[50] Consequently, roletaking aids in controlling a situation by knowing how to manipulate, direct or control others. It also, in contrast, aids societal cooperation. Cooperation can only exist when members of society are able to understand the attitudes and behaviors of other members of society. The proper amount or degree of roletaking, however, is relative and hard to isolate. Generally, individuals in higher positions of power do not require as much roletaking as those in relatively lower positions of power. Although little is known about the "amount" of roletaking, there does appear to be rather distinct types of roletaking.

Lauer and Handel have identified four types of roletaking.[51] There is, first of all, "basic roletaking." This form involves the process of constructing the perceived attitudes of others so that one may anticipate the behavior of others. "Reflexive roletaking" is adopting the role of another as a mirror which reflects the expectations and behavior of self as viewed by others. When an individual goes beyond simply constructing the attitudes of another to the internalizing and incorporating the attitude into the structure of self, the individual is engaged in "appropriative roletaking." Finally, "synesic roletaking" is a process of apprehending the feelings and perceptions of others. Here the individual is attempting to understand completely the behavior of another.

From this discussion, hopefully one sees the importance of roles. They provide the framework for interaction especially between people who have little knowledge of each other except for the roles assumed. Roles also are vitally important for assessing behavior. At the very least, roles provide models or guidelines for behavior. Some behaviors would not be acceptable for certain roles. For example, an executioner may terminate life but certainly a physician may not. The performance of roles requires, therefore: an identification of self, behavior appropriate to the identification in a situation, a background of related acts by others which serve as guidelines for behavior, and an evaluation of the role enactment. Roletaking, obviously, is largely situational. The kind of role assumed by an individual is a direct function of social context. For this reason, a consideration of the concept of situation is required.

"Mind and Society"

Behavior, as already suggested, is based on the process of examination and deliberation of a situation. In defining a situation, one must represent it to the self symbolically so that a response, hopefully appropriate, can be made. "Thus, the individual's response in any particular situation is a function of how he or she defines that situation, rather than how the situation is objectively presented to him or her."[52] Therefore, by understanding the meaning of a situation for an individual, one may understand the behavior of an individual in a specific situation.

Faules and Alexander emphasize that the process of defining a situation is not merely the labeling of perception. Rather, it is "the process of observing an event and then finding symbols to communicate the event."[53] Implicit in this notion is the assumption of an individual's creation of "reality." If people define situations as real, they are real in their consequences. The very act of defining a situation makes it become real. There can be no "crisis" until someone defines a situation as such. One may argue in 1977 that perhaps President Carter's greatest task was to convince the public that, indeed, an energy "crisis" existed.

William Thomas argues that there is always a rivalry between the spontaneous definitions of situations by individuals and definitions provided by society.[54] An individual citizen may be more hedonistic whereas society may be more utilitarian in defining situations. Because of this rivalry a moral code arises which regulates the expression of individual wishes and is built up by successive definitions of a situation. The moral code ranges from public opinion to formal written laws to religious commandments. The family functions as the smallest social unit and hence the primary defining agency followed by the general community. To complete the perspective, we must now view "society" from a symbolic interactionist viewpoint.

Historically, there has been two dominant approaches to society. Each of these approaches is too deterministic for symbolic interactionism. The sociological approach emphasizes structure. Behavior results from factors such as status position, cultural prescriptions, norms, values, social sanctions, role demands, and general system requirements. These factors are viewed as causative for behavior while ignoring social interaction which influences each of these factors. Similarly, the psychological approach emphasizes such factors as motives, attitudes, hidden complexes, and general psychological processes. Again, these factors attempt to account for behavior while ignoring the effects of social interaction. Rather than focusing on causative factors, the psychological approach focuses on the behavior such factors produce.

For symbolic interactionists, social interaction is of vital importance. Social interaction, as viewed by Blumer, "is a process that forms human conduct instead of being merely a means or a setting for the expression or release of human conduct.''[55] Thus, symbolic interactionists emphasize the dynamic, changing nature of society. Individuals are constantly interacting, developing, and shaping society. People exist in action and consequently must be viewed in terms of action. To analyze human society, the starting point must be an analysis of human beings who are engaging in action. Society, therefore, may be defined as individuals in interaction, individuals acting in relation to each other, individuals engaging in cooperative action, and people communicating with self and others. From this definition we may succinctly state that people "make" society and society "makes" people. "The activity of human beings consists of meeting a flow of situations in which they have to act and their action is built on the basis of what they note, how they assess and interpret what they note, and what kind of projected lines of action they map out.''[56]

The symbolic interactionist position rejects the notion that human society is simply an expression of pre-established forms of joint action. New situations are constantly arising requiring modification or reinforcement of existing rules of society. As Blumer notes, "it is the social process in group life that creates and upholds the rules, not the rules that create and uphold group life.''[57] Even "old" joint action arises out of a background of previous actions of the participants. Participants of any action bring unique "worlds of objects," "sets of meanings," and "schemes of interpretation." In this way, all joint action is "new" resulting from interaction although, indeed from a familiar pattern of action.

Mead identified two levels of social interaction in human society.[58] The most simple level of social interaction he called "the conversation of gestures." This form is non-symbolic interaction which occurs when one responds directly to the action of another without any interpretation of the action. The "use of significant symbols," however, involves the interpretation of an action. Non-symbolic interaction, then, is really reflex responses whereas symbolic interaction demands, in addition to some response, recognition and interpretation. To demonstrate how subtle these may be, Blumer illustrates by discussing the "responses" of a boxer.[59] When a boxer automatically raises his arm to counter a blow from an opponent, the boxer is engaged in non-symbolic interaction. If, however, the boxer identifies and interprets the blow from his opponent as a feint to trap him, symbolic interaction has occurred.

This distinction has several important implications for viewing the nature of society. Society is people acting toward one another and engaging in social interaction. The interaction is largely on the symbolic level. Group life involves defining what others do, interpreting such definitions, and, consequently, fitting one's activities to those of others.

As noted earlier, self-control is really inseparable from social-control.

The notion of "free will" is restricted and limited by the culture of an individual. The interrelationship between social-control and self-control is the result of commitment to various groups which produce a self-fulfillment, self-expression, and self-identity. Lindesmith, Strauss, and Denzin argue that there are three forms of group commitment.[60] Instrumental commitment emphasizes material benefits. One's occupational membership is an example. An emotional commitment emphasizes the personal attachment among group members. Such a commitment is best illustrated as that between a husband and wife. Finally, a moral commitment results from identification of "self" to the values or principles of a specific group. Social control is not, therefore, a matter of formal government agencies, laws, rules, and regulations. Rather, social control is a direct result of citizens identifying and internalizing the values of a group so that the values become essential to their own self-esteem and thus act so as to support the social order. Adherence to the rules of society becomes a fair price to pay for membership in the society.

To link to an earlier point, human freedom is a relative notion. Man is much more enclosed within symbolic systems than by the physical restraints of space and time. In fact, Faules and Alexander define regulation as "symbolic processes that induce change or maintain stability in self and others."[61] Of course language provides the major framework dictating ways of thinking and seeing society. Language is certainly more than the vehicle of thought. Rather, language *is* the thought. There are, however, many types or forms of symbols. Faules and Alexander argue that symbols may regulate behavior by: creating expectations, producing negative bias, or by subordinating other considerations by allowing a norm or value to supercede other symbols.[62] In short, in addition to creating expectations of behavior, symbols create social sanctions (i.e., war as God's will) or function as master symbols (i.e., to die for "freedom").

By now, the interrelationship of the terms self, role, situation, and society is evident. As a group, they provide a rather clear orientation to view the human being. The relationship of the terms is perhaps best expressed by the "father of symbolic interaction":

> ...human society is made up of individuals who have selves (that is, makes indications to themselves); that individual action is a construction and not a release, being built up by the individual through noting and interpreting features of the situations in which he acts; that group or collective action consists of the aligning of individual actions, brought about by the individuals' interpreting or taking into account each other's actions.[63]

Social organization is merely a framework within which identifiable units develop their actions. Structural features of society set conditions for action but in no way determine action.

The major assumptions, concepts, and theoretical orientations have been discussed. The task which remains is to evaluate the strengths and weaknesses of the perspective.

Symbolic Interaction as an Area of Study

Symbolic interaction, as a discipline, is a clear attempt to break away from traditional social science. The perspective focuses on human qualities and breaks away from the deterministic prison of social science. The human is viewed as maker, doer, and actor. By emphasizing the active nature of humans, the perspective questions the scientific potential for understanding human behavior. The primary goal of the perspective is the careful description of human interaction. It describes the social nature of reality, internal and external. Mead began at the level of interaction and attempted to show how social order emerges from that interaction. Social structure is constantly being modified through interaction as well as providing the context for interaction. Symbolic interaction assumes that social life can best be understood through an understanding of the perspectives of others. Consequently, the most common method employed is participant observation. The researcher is, at once, both a part of the phenomenon investigated and detached from it. The scholar directly participates in and observes the social entity under investigation.

Is symbolic interaction a method, discipline, or merely a point-of-view? The answer, of course, depends upon the respondent. As a perspective, symbolic interaction faces several criticisms.[64] The most common criticism is the general ambiguity of the perspective. The imprecise definitions lend themselves to theory rather than a body of research. In addition, the links between the interaction process and its social structural products are vague. The general lack of consensus about conceptual definitions tends to fragment the area of study.

Many scholars fault the discipline for ignoring the structures that channel the symbolic processes of individuals. Consequently, the perspective has not been utilized in the study of social organizations and institutions. Although true, recent studies are applying the notions of symbolic interaction to institutional phenomena. This study is one such example.

Somewhat related to the above criticism, symbolic interactionism fails to deal with the concept of "power" in human relationships. The perspective assumes that all individuals have equal influence in interaction. However, the interactionist does recognize the role of perception in interaction and much has been done in the area of deviance.

Finally, symbolic interactionists have ignored the emotional components of behavior. The emotions of love, hate, happiness, etc. have not been investigated as resulting from interaction.

Despite these shortcomings, symbolic interaction has several advantages.[65] First, it recognizes the importance of the symbolic processes that underlie society. Second, the concepts easily incorporate other separate considerations of interaction such as exchange theory and interpersonal communication. Furthermore, symbolic interaction encompasses the full range of human relationships. Miyamoto maintains that "...no other theory provides so admirable a social psychological basis for analyzing the problems of social organization of the processes of interpersonal relations and collective behavior."[66] As a scientific perspective, Herbert Blumer leaves little doubt about the viability of symbolic interactionism:

> It is my conviction that an empirical science necessarily has to respect the nature of the empirical world that is its object of study. In my judgement symbolic interactionism shows that respect for the nature of human group life and conduct.[67]

Conclusion

This chapter has identified and discussed the major concepts, variables, and terms of the perspective of symbolic interactionism. Human behavior must be viewed in terms of interaction. From interaction with others arises "mind," "self," and "society." Through interaction people "learn" what is "good," "bad," "right," or "wrong." In "discovering" self, one identifies, isolates, and assumes various socially defined roles. Society, therefore, is a product of a multitude of interactions that legitimize and sanction various roles which, subsequently, affect individual behavior.

In terms of this study, the next chapter is a focus on the interaction of the Presidency and the general public in attempting to isolate the various definitions and role expectations or requirements that arise from the interaction. In addition, the interaction of the office and the office holder is viewed in order to identify the "emerging" of a "Presidential self" that arises from the unique interaction. Chapter four, by focusing on the interaction of the office with society, isolates aspects of influence that the office has upon the very nature of American society and social behavior. Upon investigating these levels of interaction, one comes to a greater appreciation for the significance of the office upon society independent of its various occupants. Implications of this notion are discussed further in Chapter Five.

Footnotes

[1]Joel Charon, *Symbolic Interactionism: An Introduction, An Interpretation, An Integration* (Englewood Cliffs: Prentice-Hall, 1979), p. 3.

[2]Charon, pp. 4-8.

[3]*Ibid.,* p. 8.

[4]*Ibid.,* p. 20.

[5]Frank Miyamoto, "Self, Motivation, and Symbolic Interactionist Theory" in *Human Nature and Collective Behavior* by Tamotsu Shibutani, ed. (Englewood Cliffs: Prentice-Hall, 1970), p. 271.

[6]Randall Collins, "Interpretive Social Psychology" in *Symbolic Interaction: A Reader in Social Psychology* by Jerome Manis and Bernard Meltzer, eds. (Boston: Allyn and Bacon, 1978), p. 397.

[7]Collins, p. 397.

[8]Herbert Blumer, "Society as Symbolic Interaction" in *Symbolic Interaction: A Reader in Social Psychology* by Jerome Manis and Bernard Meltzer, eds. (Boston: Allyn and Bacon, 1978), p. 96.

[9]Herbert Blumer, *Symbolic Interactionism* (Englewood Cliffs: Prentice-Hall, 1969), p. 66.

[10]Blumer, *Symbolic Interactionism,* p. 66.

[11]*Ibid,* p. 47.

[12]*Ibid.,* p. 50.

[13]*Ibid.,* p. 49.

[14]*Ibid.,* p. 48.

[15]Alfred Lindesmith, Anselm Strauss, and Norman Denzin, *Social Psychology* (Illinois: Dryden Press, 1975), p. 4.

[16]Charon, p. 28.

[17]*Ibid.*

[18]Robert Lauer and Warren Handel, *Social Psychology: The Theory and Application of Symbolic Interaction* (Boston: Houghton Mifflin, 1977), p. 15.

[19]Charon, p. 28.

[20]See Bernard Meltzer and John Petras, "The Chicago and Iowa Schools of Symbolic Interactionism" in *Human Nature and Collective Behavior* by Tomotsu Shibutani, ed. (Englewood Cliffs: Prentice-Hall, 1970), pp. 6-14 and B. Meltzer, J. Petras, and L. Reynolds, "Varieties of Symbolic Interactionism" in *Symbolic Interaction: A Reader in Social Psychology* by Jerome Manis and Bernard Meltzer, ed. (Boston: Allyn and Bacon, 1978), pp. 41-56.

[21]Meltzer and Petras, p. 6.

[22]*Ibid.,* p. 7.

[23]*Ibid.,* p. 14.

[24]Lauer and Handel, p. 41.

[25]*Ibid.,* p. 43.

[26]*Ibid.,* p. 41.

[27]Blumer, *Symbolic Interaction,* p. 10-12.

[28]*Ibid.,* p. 10.

[29]*Ibid.,* p. 12.

[30]George H. Mead, *Mind, Self, and Society* (Chicago: University of Chicago Press, 1972), p. 122.

[31]Charon, p. 40.

[32]Don Faules and Dennis Alexander, *Communication and Social Behavior: A Symbolic Interaction Perspective* (Mass.: Addison-Wesley Publishing, 1978), p. 17.

[33]Faules and Alexander, p. 92.

[34]Orrin E. Klapp, *Symbolic Leaders* (Chicago: Aldine, 1964).

[35]See Peter Hall, "A Symbolic Interactionist Analysis of Politics," *Sociological Inquiry,* 42 (3-4), 1972, 35-74.

[36]Blumer, *Symbolic Interaction,* p. 2.

[37]*Ibid.*

[38]*Ibid.*

[39]Lauer and Handel, p. 34. Their definition comes from Sanford Labovitz and Robert Hagedorn, *Introduction to Social Research* (New York: McGraw-Hill, 1971), p. 18.

[40]William James, "The Social Self," in *Social Psychology Through Symbolic Interaction* by Gregory Stone and Harvey Farberman, eds. (Mass.: Ginn-Blaisdell, 1970), p. 374.

[41]Mead, pp. 135-222.

[42]*Ibid.,* p. 138.

[43]*Ibid.,* p. 149.

[44]These characteristics are based on those provided by Lauer and Handel, pp. 67-70.

[45]Lauer and Handel, p. 67.

[46]*Ibid.,* p. 68.

[47]Faules and Alexander, p. 61.

[48]Blumer, *Symbolic Interaction,* p. 13.

[49]Hans Gerth and C. Wright Mills, "Institutions and Persons" in *Symbolic Interaction: A Reader in Social Psychology* by Jerome Manis and Bernard Meltzer, eds. (Boston: Allyn and Bacon, 1978), p. 117.

[50]Lauer and Handel, p. 60.

[51]*Ibid.,* pp. 62-63.

[52]*Ibid.,* p. 85.

[53]Faules and Alexander, p. 167.

[54]Manis and Meltzer, p. 255.

[55]Blumer, *Symbolic Interaction,* p. 8.

[56]*Ibid.,* p. 16.

[57]*Ibid.,* p. 19.

[58]The discussion of these two levels of social interaction occur throughout the work *Mind, Self, and Society* but especially see pp. 13-18, 61-68, 253-260.

[59]Blumer, *Symbolic Interaction,* p. 8.

[60]Lindesmith, Strauss, and Denzin, p. 430.

[61]Faules and Alexander, p. 130.

[62]*Ibid.,* p. 140.

[63]Blumer, *Symbolic Interaction,* p. 99.

[64]For good discussion of faults see Lauer and Handel, pp. 142-172 as well as Manis and Meltzer, pp. 437-440.

[65]A good review is Jonathan Turner, "Symbolic Interactionism and Social Organization" in *Symbolic Interaction: A Reader in Social Psychology* by Jerome Manis and Bernard Meltzer, eds. (Boston: Allyn and Bacon, 1978), pp. 400-401.

[66]Miyamoto, p. 272.

[67]Blumer, *Symbolic Interaction,* p. vii.

Chapter 3

"Mind" and the Emerging of the "Presidential Self"

Introduction

Within academe, the "territorial borders" of subject matter are as well protected and fought over as the boundaries of any nation. Each discipline carves out a "chunk" and further sub-divides the subject into "areas of concentration." Consequently, the world is presented in simple dichotomies. For every question there is an answer. For every judgment there is an opinion. One is either a political leader or follower, active or passive, opinion leader or follower. One's motives are either sociologically determined by environment and social class or rooted in psychological traits of personality.[1] Although increasing, inter-disciplinary approaches to social phenomena and the sharing of perspectives should be encouraged. The concept of "roles" from social psychology can be most useful to the scholar of politics.[2] Yet, in the past, political scientists have failed to recognize fully the dynamic, "process" nature of the concept.

Most political scientists recognize that the Presidency is both an institution and a role. As such, the Presidency has a great deal of influence upon those who occupy the office as well as upon the general public. Historians, when studying the relationship between Presidents and the Presidency, usually focus on the growth of Presidential power. Political scientists, specifically, tend to emphasize individual Presidents' use of power. Power, therefore, is viewed as the "heart" of the Presidency or at least the "heart"

37

of strong leadership. Scholars, in relation to the Presidency, have been obsessed with the end result or product of power. Consequently, traditional political approaches to Presidential roles or models of the Presidency are attempts to view the nature and functioning of Presidential power. But in investigating power, one is led to many areas of study and questions. *What* is power? *Where* is power? *How* does one *obtain* power? *When* should one use power? Although all these questions deal with the "nature" of power, some scholars focus on such diverse topics as: constitutional law, the nature of society, socialization, personality theory, management theory, persuasion, and decision making. For the symbolic interactionist, however, power is neither the "beginning" nor the "end all" of the study of relationships and institutions. Power, as will be discussed later, as with beauty, is in the eyes of the beholder.

Political roles are not concrete, static entities. Rather, they are ideas about what people expect to do in certain situations as well as what others expect them to do in certain situations. While the concept of role does deal with ultimate behavior, it *is not* the activity of behavior itself. The distinction between what individuals think they should do and what in fact they do should not be ignored. As Long notes:

> The actors in the world of politics are neither the rational calculators of economic man nor the uncultured savages of Hobbe's state of nature but are born into a political culture, albeit frequently an ambiguous one, and are socialized to a range of response patterns that may be invoked by diverse stimuli. With this equipment, they confront a reality that seems to each public, one-dimensional common sense but, in fact, through the differing glasses that it is viewed, presents widely differing perspectives.[3]

Political actors, therefore, possess a "repertory of responses" or roles. Upon any stimulus, the appropriate role behavior is a product of what the actor perceives the defined role to be which also fulfills the expectations of the public. "The existence of these patterned sets of roles is part of the technology of the political culture and permits the actors to function with the same ease as a ballplayer playing his position."[4] Thus, roles (political or otherwise) are comprised of internal and external elements.[5] The former consists of the individual's own perception of what a task demands and how to fulfill it. The latter are the expectations and orientations of members of society. However, as Haight and Johnston point out:

> ...the division into roles can be deceptive...and one must never forget the fact that one man plays all the parts. The President can never separate his problems and divide them into preconceived categories for decision. Each decision will involve the President as a whole man, and he will need in some manner to accommodate several often conflicting roles in order to determine a course of action.[6]

This chapter, therefore, differs from traditional treatment of Presidential roles. The dynamic, "process," and evolutionary aspects of Presidential roles will be emphasized which is more congruent with role theory as espoused in social psychology.

As noted in Chapter 2, the nature of *interaction* is key to symbolic interaction theory. Through interaction, "meaning" develops and "reality" is created. In addition, the nature of "reality" is largely symbolic. This chapter will focus on two dimensions or levels of interaction. First, the interaction of the office of President with the public is investigated in order to reveal the emergence of the American "Presidential self." Such investigation ultimately considers:

1. various types of Presidential roles that have developed throughout history,
2. various expectations of Presidential behavior and job performance that have evolved from the emergence of the roles, and
3. how Presidential roles are created, sustained, and permeated over time resulting in, what appears to be, the mythic, paradoxical development of the office.

Second, the chapter views the interaction of the office with the office holder. This level of interaction reveals the unique and even stressful adaptation of an individuals's self perceptions to the perceived role requirements of the institution. More specifically, this level of interaction considers:

1. the "process" of the individual evaluating "self" against the perceived demands and expectations of the office,
2. the "process" of adapting oneself to the office which clearly entails more than simply taking the oath of office, and
3. the distinct and possible harmful consequences, as exemplified in the Johnson and Nixon administrations, of the transformation process of "becoming" President.

The next chapter will be a discussion of the interaction of the Presidency and society as related to social control and societal behavior.

Presidential Functions, Roles, and Models

What *is* the American Presidency? What is the *essence* of the office? In attempting to answer these questions, one is easily confronted with a multitude of answers. The answers, however, often appear contradictory and vast indeed. Woe to the fabled "martian" who asks the above questions. For there seems to be as many responses as there are respondents. Generally, when one thinks of the Presidency, one envisions a "favorite" office holder, a laundry list of duties, or a specific orientation to power necessary to fulfill the requirements of the office.

In reviewing the literature on the Presidency, one notices three distinct approaches to describing the office. Scholars often refer to Presidential functions, roles, and models. Yet, these terms are often used interchangeably and hence, ambiguously. But the differences, although subtle, are important, for each notion differs in the creation of public expectations and the mythic development of the office. In addition, for purposes of this chapter, does the public "interact" with Presidential functions, roles, or models? The public *reacts* and *interacts* with Presidential roles. If the public (or scholar) likes the role set of the occupant, then "a" model of Presidential performance is established independent of functions. This notion will become more clear after considering the differences among Presidential functions, roles, and models.

A function is the specific, natural action or activity of something. Politically, functions are the special duties or actions required of someone in an occupation or office. Certainly related, a role is a part or "character" assumed by an individual. A model is a pattern, example, or standard that can be used for comparison or even imitation. From these brief characterizations, functions are viewed as the specific duties regardless of orientation, roles, or models. One may select the "best" model or most "appropriate" role to achieve specific functions. Presidential functions are generic, job descriptions of tasks to be performed. Presidential roles are more specific. They are the medium to carry out specific actions, duties, or functions. Presidential models are unique orientations to carrying out roles and functions of the office. Models, in this context, may be thought of as "types of presidencies." Thus, Presidential functions transcend individual Presidents. They are specific and offer little choice as to fulfillment. An individual President, however, may assume many different roles to carry out or to complete the functions required. As will be seen, many factors may influence role selection; several roles, at different times, may be required to fulfill one function. Finally, a patterned set of roles may produce a model or general orientation to fulfilling Presidential functions. Models, perhaps, is the most general, broad, and flexible of the concepts.

Before an investigation of the "interaction" of the office with the public can occur, a review of the various Presidential functions, roles, and models is required. Such a review is vital for appreciation of the expectations of the public that result from such characterizations and how these expectations are created, sustained, and permeated in society.

Presidential Functions

As noted elsewhere, Article II of the Constitution dealing with the Presidency is vague and sketchy. In fact, of all the major clauses in the Constitution, the one governing the Presidency is the shortest. The members of the Constitutional Convention did not delineate in great detail the powers and responsibilities of the Presidency. According to Rossiter, eight key decisions were made at different times throughout the convention which created the form and structure of the American Presidency:[7]

1. A separate executive office should be established apart from the legislature.
2. The executive office should consist of one man to be called the President of the United States.
3. The President should be elected apart from the legislature.
4. The executive office should have a fixed term subject to termination by conviction of impeachment for high crimes or misdemeanors.
5. The President should be eligible for re-election with no limit as to the number of terms.
6. The President should derive power from the Constitution and not simply from Congress.
7. The President should not be encumbered with a specified body to seek approval for nominations, vetos, or other acts. And
8. As President, one may not be a member of either house of Congress.

These "key" decisions created the office, but they contain little information as to what the office entails. Nearly half of Article II simply deals with tenure, qualifications, and election of the President. Section 2 of Article II states that the President "shall be Commander in Chief," "shall have power to grant reprieves and pardons," "make treaties, provided two-thirds of the Senators present concur," "appoint Ambassadors, other public Ministers and Consuls, Judges of the Supreme Court, and all other officers of the United States...by and with the advice and consent of the Senate" and "shall have power to fill all vacancies that may happen during the recess of the Senate." Section 3 adds that the President "shall from time to time give to the Congress information of the State of the Union," "convene both Houses...on extraordinary occasions," "shall receive Ambassadors and other public Ministers" and "shall take care that the laws be faithfully executed."[8] These, then, are the duties as specified in the Constitution. On the surface, they appear rather simple and straightforward. It is the fulfilling of these functions that complicates the office.

Contemporary scholars, when addressing Presidential functions, seldom delineate constitutional provisions. Rather, they group Presidential tasks into broad, general categories. These categories, of course, differ in number. For Cronin, the job description of the President involves six major functions:[9]

1. Symbolic leadership which must generate hope, confidence, national purpose.
2. Setting national priorities and designing programs which will receive public attention and a legislative hearing.
3. Crisis management which has become increasingly important since 1940.
4. Constant legislative and political coalition building.
5. Program implementation and evaluation which has also become increasingly difficult in modern times. And
6. General oversight of government routines which forces the President to be responsible for governmental performance at all levels.

Somewhat related to Cronin, Buchanan identifies four "generic" functions of the Presidency: national symbol, policy advocate, mediator among national interests, and crisis manager.[10] Reedy believes, however, that what a President must do can be boiled down to two simple fundamentals: "He must resolve the policy questions that will not yield to quantitative, empirical analysis; and he must persuade enough of his countrymen of the rightness of his decisions so that he can carry them out without destroying the fabric of society."[11]

From this brief discussion of Presidential functions, the constitution as a job description is vague and general. A President clearly "does" more than what is outlined in the Constitution. Even as Commander-in-Chief, the President may undertake crisis management, legislative and political coalition building, etc. It is *how* one meets or carries out the functions that provide insight into how the institution influences behavior.

Presidential Roles

Edwin Corwin was the first to mention Presidential roles as sources of power.[12] A President's power is based upon five Constitutional roles: Chief of State, Chief Executive, Chief Diplomat, Commander-in-Chief, and Chief Legislator. These roles are roughly analogous to the various areas of responsibilities outlined in the Constitution. A President who creates additional roles and hence additional power approaches a dangerous "personalization of the office."

As Chief of State, the President functions as the ceremonial head of government not unlike the monarchy of England. Some would argue that the majority of Presidential activity is ceremonial. Projected upon the President is the symbol of sovereignty, continuity, and grandeur. As Chief

Executive, the President is manager of one of the largest "corporations" in the world. Whether the President likes it or not, he is held responsible for the quality of governmental performance ranging from a simple letter of complaint to military preparedness. In event of war, the President as Commander-in-Chief must ensure strategic execution and victory. Within modern history, the field of foreign relations has become extremely important. The formulation of foreign policy and the conduct of foreign affairs forces the President to serve as the nation's Chief Diplomat. Finally, by providing domestic leadership, the President must guide Congress by identifying national priorities for legislation. These "legitimate," Constitution roles are obviously interrelated. Yet, the various "hats" require rather distinct approaches, strategies, and temperament. Even these, however, may be situationally bound.

Clinton Rossiter, building on Corwin's analyses argues that five extra-constitutional roles must be recognized: Chief of Party, Protector of the Peace, Manager of Prosperity, World Leader, and Voice of the People.[13] Rossiter, as Corwin, believes that the source of Presidential power lies in the combination of the various roles. Rossiter, at least, recognizes the "expanding" nature of the Presidency. These extra roles resulted from the growing activities of a President plus the growing expectations of the public. As Hale has succinctly stated, "roles became obligations and duties, as each role became a Presidential responsibility."[14] When speaking of Presidential roles, most scholars cite Rossiter's classic *The American Presidency*. Hence, the list of roles is fairly stationary. Yet, as the functions or duties of the Presidency grow, so do the roles. As the various tasks become more complex, numerous roles may be required to carry out one function. One should also note that each role may require very different skills and techniques. Roles, then, are more "numerous" than functions. They are labels or "characters" that people see and each has a distinct "mode" usually congruent with public expectations which will be developed later. Finally, if a role set is "good" or "successful," the set may become a model. The model may thus serve as an overall approach to the fulfillment of the functions. The role set, as a model, may be praised, condemned, imitated or serve as a guide to performance.

Presidential Models

Presidential models, of course, as of 1980 are only based upon thirty-six individuals. Models tend to develop from a number of individuals sharing similar approaches to the tasks of the job or formulated on an individual President altering from traditional approaches to the Presidency. Consequently, Presidential models are general orientations to the job as President of the United States.

There appears to be three basic types of Presidential models. The first type is based upon individual Presidential performances. These often characterize how an individual President viewed the office and performed the various tasks and roles. The most frequently mentioned "individual" Presidential models include: Hamilton, Jefferson, Madison, Buchanan, Lincoln, and Cleveland. The Madisonian model is named after the "father of the Constitution."[15] This model closely reflects the "hopes and expectations" of the members of the Constitutional Convention. The Madisonian model emphasizes four major concepts. First, the model fully supports the notion of "checks and balances." Each branch of government has recognized powers and specified "advantages" over the other branches. Second, this model values minority rights. In fact, one of the major purposes of the system of checks and balances is to protect the rights of minority groups or interests. Consequently, anti-majoritarianism also characterizes this model. The Presidency is structured to prevent "tyrannical" majorities from obtaining control of the government. Finally, the model reflects a conservative, prudent, limited view of the role of government in society. John Adams was the first President to attempt to operate under the theoretical assumptions of the model.

The Jeffersonian model is somewhat more daring than the Madisonian Presidential model.[16] The Jeffersonian model reflects a unified political system. Political parties ultimately control the machinery of government which lessens the impact of "checks and balances." The President, as party leader, governs from a mandate of the voters who have competitively evaluated the various platforms and issues of the candidates. Thus, although the model assumes a "vigorous and vocal" minority, majority rule is at the heart of this model.

The Hamiltonian model, in some respects, is a mixture of the previous two models.[17] Thus, it is somewhat more difficult to define. Above all, the model demands "heroic leadership" from the President. The President is viewed as the primary "mover" and "doer" in establishing national goals and priorities. Hence, the role of the party is less significant and the individual President must rely heavily on a "personal organization" built up over many years to perform his required tasks. The emphasis, therefore, is on national leadership, expedient use of power, and constant thwarting of the efforts of opposition party leadership.

These three models, historically, encompass the various approaches to Presidential functions and powers. In some cases, these models serve as beginning points for the development of other models of Presidential authority which will be viewed later. Their comparative nature is succinctly characterized by James Burns:

> If the Hamiltonian model implied a federal government revolving
> around the Presidency, and depending on energy, resourcefulness,

inventiveness, and a ruthless pragmatism in the executive office; and if the Madisonian model implied a prudent, less daring and active government, one that was balanced between the legislative and executive forces and powers, the Jeffersonian model was almost revolutionary, implying government by majority rule, under strong Presidential leadership, with a highly competitive two-party system and with a more popular, democratic, and egalitarian impetus than the Madisonians.[18]

Interestingly, the only other major Presidential models named after individual office holders generally reflect the above models. Sidney Hyman identifies three models of Presidential performance in response to the question: "What is the President's true role?"[19] The Buchanan concept, according to Hyman, views the Presidency as simply an "administrative office." The President should not be the major political leader of the nation. Rather, "the main function of the President is to be efficient, honest, decorous, pious."[20] The Lincoln concept makes the office much more political in nature. The President is viewed as leader of the nation: legislatively, economically, and morally. "It looks upon partisan politics as a creative instrument that can define and, to some extent at least, resolve things in dispute."[21] Finally, the Cleveland concept of the Presidency "shuttles" between those above. Thus, this model is merely a mixture of the Lincoln and Buchanan concepts.

Models based on individual Presidents have a serious flaw. Two Presidents may view themselves as "strong" and "powerful" yet both may execute their jobs differently. Thus, the issue of a President believing that the job requires "strength" and becoming "strong" is ignored. In short, individual models of the Presidency ignore "quality" differences. The second type of Presidential models, discussed below, attempts to address this dimension.

Pious, in *The American Presidency,* identifies four models of the Presidency of which two are more prevalent.[22] The Benevolent President is one who is nominated by party regulars, elected by a popular majority, and bases programs on the party platform. This President accepts democratic values and relies on persuasion to elicit support. In contrast, the Malevolent President is one nominated by manipulation of special interest groups, attempts to centralize power, and exhibits "imperial" tendencies. In addition, this President does not internalize democratic values and relies on command rather than persuasion to elicit cooperation. Of lesser importance is the Co-Opted President. Here, the real center of power lies within an "elite" group of individuals recruited from major corporations, the military, and universities. This "elite" group of people virtually makes all crucial decisions. Finally, Pious recognizes the Amateur President. This President is passive, non-political, and functions primarily as a "prime minister." "He presides over the government but does not run it."[23]

Even these models tend to overlap and blend depending upon issues, situations, and length in office. The most recent types of Presidential models are those which present very dichotomous approaches to the office. Although the most broad and general of the models, they trace the office historically as well as reflect the views of the office by contemporary authors. The two most frequently identified models of the Presidency today are the "White Knight" versus "Black Hat" and "liberal" versus "conservative." The former reflects the debate found in textbooks about the nature of the office and the latter focuses on the question of Presidential power.

The "liberal versus conservative" model stems from the Hamiltonian and Madisonian models.[24] As already mentioned, the Madisonian model is based primarily on the notion of separation of powers. In addition, the role of government and, consequently, Presidential power is restricted. This model of Presidential power and influence has become known as the "conservative" model which existed primarily from 1864 to 1932. This period has been labeled "the main stream of Congressional government."

The "liberal" model of the Presidency is based on the Hamiltonian model. Here, the focus is on executive power and strong leadership. Because of the increasing complexity of the world and rising expectations, the power and influence of the Presidency has continued to grow. This resulted in a shift of leadership from the legislative to the executive branch. Hamilton, Jefferson, Jackson, Lincoln, Theodore Roosevelt, Wilson, and Franklin Roosevelt all contributed to the development of the "liberal" model. Certainly, in more recent times, the Johnson and Nixon administrations epitomize the "liberal" model.

More recent Presidential scholars are recognizing two rather dichotomous models coming from "textbooks" of the 1960's and 1970's.[25] One view espouses the need for strong leadership to guide the nation while the other warns of an "imperial Presidency." Authors during the 1950's created a "larger-than-life" image of the Presidency. The textbooks stressed the growing nature of the office in terms of responsibilities and emphasized the importance of personal attributes of the individuals. Thus, the task was simply to select the right man or "White Knight" for the job. Thomas Cronin offers four concise propositions which best characterizes this model of the presidency.[26] Two of the propositions emphasize the dimension of omnipotence and the others emphasize the benevolent dimension.

1. Omnipotent-Competent Dimension:
    A. The President is the strategic catalyst for progress in the American political system and the central figure in the international system as well.

    B. Only the President can be the genuine architect of U.S.
public policy, and only he, by attacking problems frontally
and aggressively and by interpreting his power expansively,
can slay the dragons of crisis and be the engine of change to
move the nation forward.

2. Moralistic-Benevolent Dimension:

    C. The President must be the nation's personal and moral leader;
by symbolizing the past and future greatness of America and
radiating inspirational confidence, a President can pull the
nation together while directing its people toward fulfillment
of the American Dream.

    D. If, and only if, the right person is placed in the White House,
all will be well; and, somehow, whoever is in the White
House is the best person for the job—at least for a year or
so.

Many crises of leadership during the 1970's developed. As Presidential
powers increased so did the magnitude of failure. Among the most important crises were: Bay of Pigs, racial problems, urban decay, pollution,
Vietnam, Watergate, and rampant inflation. As the quality of society was
threatened, so was the "White Knight" model of the Presidency. Scholars
began questioning not only the expansive powers and influence of the Presidency but the very nature of the office. Were Johnson and Nixon merely
accidents of "White Knights" becoming "Black Hats" or had the institution become structurally defective? There may be many answers to this
question. Perhaps one answer lies in the exaggerated perceptions and
expectations of the institution which is not congruent with the "reality" of
the nature of man or the world community.

The purpose of viewing Presidential functions, roles, and models here
was to appreciate the subtle differences of each. Most roles and models
emphasize a variety of "approaches" to relatively few "generic" functions
of the office. As the Presidency becomes more complex, so do the models
and the number of roles. Correspondingly, as the number of roles increase
so do expectations of Presidential performance. Microscopically, I would
posit that each "classic role" dictates a unique rhetorical style and
approach. The roles, then, not only establish unique rhetorical constraints
but also create specific rhetorical expectations over time with the public.

Role Expectations

A "role set" is a set of "behavioral relationships that exist between
positions."[27] Borden, Gregg, and Grove argue that there are two kinds of

role sets.[28] Traditional role sets refer to institutionalized relationships such as husband and wife, lawyer and client, etc. These role sets, therefore, provide general guidelines for behavior. Traditional role sets serve primarily task-maintenance functions whereas unique role sets serve primarily person-maintenance functions. Thus, traditional role sets provide already established interaction patterns and set up general expectations of the participants.

Certainly, the American Presidency has established a rather clear traditional role set. The title of President implies more than simply a job description. To know that a person is President is to know in a very general way how the individual is likely to behave and how others will behave toward the individual. The title not only provides a means for anticipating a range of behaviors, but also confines the range of behaviors possible. Thus, behavioral expectations and restrictions are attached to all social positions. Richard Ross notes that "empirical investigations usually reveals that leaders are often constrained by the expectations of their followers and in some cases compelled to follow their followers or risk deposition as leader."[29]

Cronin recognizes that a basic tendency of Americans is to believe in great personages, "...that someone, somewhere, can and will cope with the major crises of the present and future."[30] Within our society, the Presidency fulfills this need and becomes the symbol of our hopes. Presidents are more likely, historically, to be placed on a "pedestal" than under a "microscope." Although this tendency is acknowledged by political scientists, Cronin insists that the discipline has "...usually not read in such meaning, or at least have not infused their view of the Presidency with connotations of a civil religion."[31] Consequently, simply to speak of Presidential functions in no way adequately describes what the Presidency "really is."

Emmet Hughes, in *The Living Presidency* which is certainly of the "White Knight" orientation, states that a President faces two constituencies: "the living citizens and the future historians."[32] This certainly is not an easy task. Nearly all scholars agree that any American President inherits a vast, complex set of role expectations. "The fact that there are many roles involved in the most important political office gives a politician the discretion of deciding which to emphasize and which to ignore. He can, at the least, choose what he ignores."[33] But such choice is not a one way street. Roles create expectations but societal expectations can create political roles. As Murray Edelman perceptively notes:

> ...expectations also evoke a specific political role and self-conception for those individuals who accept the myth in question: the patriotic soldier whose role it is to sacrifice, fight, and die for his country; the policeman or National Guardsman whose role it is to save the social order from subhuman or radical hordes....[34]

For Edelman, the degree of attachment to a political myth and the role it creates plus the fervor with which the role is acted out depend upon "the degree of anxiety the myth rationalizes, and the intensity with which the particular expectation that forms the central premise of the myth is held."[35] When Alfred de Grazia speaks of "the myth of the President," he is referring to "a number of qualities [that] are given to every President that are either quite fictitious or large exaggerations of the real man."[36] He further notes that "the myth is not alone the property of the untutored mind, but of academicians, scientists, newspapermen, and even Congressmen."[37]

Thus, the office of the Presidency has grown because of *interaction*; interaction of the office with the public and the public with the office. As public expectations increase, so does the job. Concurrently, the job is forced to expand to meet public expectations.

Types of Expectations

As already mentioned, there appears to be a growth in public expectations of the Presidency. However, Twentieth Century Presidents, because of the use of mass media, have encouraged the public to identify with the candidate and potential of the office. Consequently, the public has responded by holding the President accountable for meeting various demands. David Easton has identified two types of expectations that citizens have of political leadership.[38] One focuses on the office and the other focuses on the individual who holds the office. Diffuse support is "...an attachment to a political object for its own sake, it constitutes a store of political goodwill. As such it taps deep political sentiments."[39] Specific support "flows from the favorable attitudes and predispositions stimulated by outputs that are perceived by members to meet their demands as they arise..."[40] The question as to which type of support is more prevalent in regards to the Presidency is difficult to answer. A study by Seligman and Baer, however, concluded that "...the situation influenced expectations more than the occupant of the Presidency."[41] For the purposes of this study, both types of public expectations will be explored.

A. *Diffuse support*

An individual President is the embodiment of our nation. As Brownlow argues, each citizen, therefore, "identifies the President with his own private and particular notion of what this nation is and what Americans are."[42] If this is true, one may further argue that there are as many different specific expectations of Presidential performance as there are citizens because no two citizens share the same visions of national being or national destiny.

Without doubt, however, the President is the best known American political figure. A national survey in 1970 revealed that 98 percent of the adult population could identify the incumbent President.[43] In addition, even 94 percent of those of age 13 could name the incumbent President.

Also without question is the fact that the Presidency is accorded a great deal of respect in our society. The office ranks first choice among Americans as the kind of job respected highly when surveyed by the University of Michigan Research Center.[44] In fact, a poll taken in May of 1973 when the Watergate controversy placed Nixon's popularity at a near record low, the Presidency itself remained in relatively high esteem.[45]

Although well known and generally respected, the office can come under harsh criticism.[46] As Bishop notes in referring to the Johnson years:

> He has become the dispenser of all good and evil. The quality of these adjectives is determined by the people. They may withhold applause when his work is good, but they never fail to hiss his blunders. Public scrutiny of the office, and every act of the President, is what makes the position impossible today.[47]

Generally, most Presidential scholars, although using somewhat different terminology, believe that the American people expect three major aspects of Presidential behavior.[48] First, the President is expected to be a competent manager of the vast machinery of government. Second, the American people expect the President to take care of their needs by initiating programs, legislation, and safeguarding the economy. Finally, the people want a sense of legitimacy from the President. The office, while providing symbolic affirmation of the nation's values, should faithfully represent the opinions of the public as well.

B. *Specific Presidential Characteristics*

What type of person should be President of the United States? What qualities should one have for the job? On the surface, these seem to be legitimate questions. Scholars and citizens alike have confronted the issue. Indeed, judgment is required at least every four years. Simple surveys easily produce a "laundry list" of desired Presidential qualities, a very demanding list to be sure. It is much more difficult, however, to isolate the roots of such qualities. Are desired Presidential qualities founded in history, myth, and merely perpetuated through textbooks? The implications of the answer to such a question are important.

Rossiter, in his classic work, identified seven qualities "that a man must have or cultivate if he is to be an effective modern President."[49] First, a President must have bounce; "that extra elasticity, given to few men, which makes it possible for him to thrive on the toughest diet of work and responsibility of the world."[50] In addition, the Presidency demands affability, political skill, cunning, a sense of history, the newspaper habit ("must be on guard least be cut off from harsh reality"), and a sense of humor. Such qualities, I am sure, are indeed needed. I also think, however, that they would be an asset for one contemplating pursuing a Ph.D. degree. And certainly Presidents of major corporations should probably likewise be so characterized.

Hughes' *The Living Presidency*, also of a "White Knight" orientation, prefers to address qualities that "shapes and makes an effective Presidential style."[51] Such a style includes:

1. A sense of confidence; "...with no harm to his leadership so grave as a show of hesitation."
2. A sense of proportion; "the avoidance of excess and extravagance."
3. A sense of drama; "...a truly important Presidency has never failed to raise the noise and dust of combat."
4. A sense of timing; "...sure instinct for pace and rhythm."
5. A sense of constancy; "With no necessary loss of popular trust, he may vary his methods, but he must not appear to vary or to waiver."
6. A sense of humanity; "...humility and humor, and toward the people, with warmth and compassion."
7. A sense of perspective; "...no saving quality that a President may lose more swiftly upon entering the White House..."
8. And above all, a sense of history.

Such an approach is more profitable. It provides more of a guideline to Presidential performance than a list of specific qualities.

Another way to ascertain the qualities a President should have is to confront those who have worked closely with Presidents. They not only know the qualities of specific Presidents but also know the demands of the job. Many of their assessments, however, are equally as vague and disappointing.

Sherman Adams, a key figure in the Eisenhower Administration, believes that the two qualities vital to the success of any President are "intellectual receptivity and the instinct to recognize his own prejudice or bias."[52] Clark Clifford, counselor to Truman, Kennedy, and Secretary of Defense for Johnson, cites in order of importance the qualities of "character, intellect, decisiveness, political understanding, and awareness of the potential of the office."[53] Theodore Sorensen, a close aid to John Kennedy, believes that the personal qualities of judgment and leadership are the most important.[54] How does one "measure" the qualities? What *is* "character" and "leadership?" In terms of intellect, one is reminded of a quip by Homes: "For a President can always hire brains. But there is no way for him to lease fortitude or borrow intuition."[55] Yet, how does one "develop" intuition? More importantly, how does one "measure" intuition during a campaign?

Perhaps a better approach in attempting to view the qualities a President should have is to view the characteristics of specific popular Presidents and to view specific behaviors the public would oppose. A Gallup poll conducted in 1980 asked respondents, "Of all the Presidents we've ever had, who do you wish were President today?"[56] The results revealed in order of preference: John Kennedy, Franklin Roosevelt, Harry Truman, Dwight Eisenhower, Abraham Lincoln, Gerald Ford, Richard Nixon, Theodore Roosevelt, Jimmy Carter, and Lyndon Johnson. Even these results are suspect. Are Jimmy Carter or Gerald Ford really better Presidents than Washington, Jefferson, or Jackson? Did Kennedy really provide more unity, leadership, and legislation than did Franklin Roosevelt or even Lyndon Johnson? Thus, before these results are useful, one must know the specific qualities possessed that caused individuals to be ranked highly. It appears that one simply needed to be a somewhat recent President and a product of some historical myth building.

The general public is rather clear, however, on what they *do not* want a President to do. A recent national survey by Gallup found that:[57]

70% oppose a President smoking marijuana
43% object to a President telling racial or ethnic jokes
38% object to a President not belonging to a church
36% object to a President occasionally using tranquilizers
33% object to a President using profanity
30% object to a President having seen a psychiatrist
21% object to a President wearing jeans in the oval office
17% object to a President being divorced
14% object to a President having a cocktail

Although some of the percentages appear to be rather low, scholars generally agree that if as few as 33 percent of the public objects to any practice, a candidate's chances of election are very slim. The survey also revealed that 74% *would not* vote for an atheist. Interestingly, only 58 percent thought a divorced individual could be elected, 40 percent a Jew could be elected, 37 percent a Black could be elected, and a mere 33 percent a woman could be elected.

What can be surmised from such diverse lists of desired Presidential qualities? First, they are largely "useless." The qualities may be characterized as admirable, often contradictory, general, abstract, and even "biblical." Many have no direct relationship to job or task performance. As a result, secondly, the question becomes whether the public imposes these qualities on the President or do Presidents create the impressions of meeting these qualities. Clearly, the answer is both. As a result of the interaction, when Presidents "appear" to meet the desired qualities, then the qualities become embedded as part of the public's expectations. Finally, the desired qualities often reflect individual senses of "goodness," "morality," ideas of "right" and "wrong." Individuals may occasionally drink but be appalled at such behavior from their ministers. Consequently, it is not surprising that the public desires Presidents "not to do as the citizens do, but what they say to do." There is no test that Presidential candidates take to reveal true intelligence, integrity, a sense of history, etc. They are simply forced to demonstrate through campaigning that they, in fact, are intelligent, honest, knowledgeable, etc. Hence the qualities are in the "mind" and largely depend upon "perception" as to their reality.

The last of this chapter will confront the "crisis" of individual Presidents attempting to meet the "qualities" and expectations of the public. For now, the nature of such expectations and their impact upon the office must be appreciated. As Howard K. Smith observes:

> They don't define what they want very clearly, but they think they know it when they see it. The ability to communicate a sense of action that lifts the heart, as John Kennedy did. The visibility of massive action against an array of distresses that FDR thrilled the nation with. The "rock-like" insistence on doing what's right and not what's popular that made people angry at Truman in office, but saved the free world and made a hero of him in retrospect.[58]

Consequences of Expectations

The simple truth is that the nation expects more from the President than either the authority or the means allows one to provide. In fact, about 75 percent of the American people, when questioned, admit that their expectations are unfairly high.[59] One man simply cannot keep the economy at a high level, decrease unemployment, and stop inflation. No man can guarantee, in this world, a life of peace, contentment, and security. As Sidney Hyman notes: "He does not have God's autonomous powers to make mountains without valleys as the mood strikes him."[60] Consequently, "the difference between what some of us imagine the Presidency to be and what it really is leads to disappointment, frustration, and attack."[61] Thus, expecting the impossible from a President inevitably leads to disappointment in his performance.

But disappointment in Presidential performance is not the only consequence of false expectations. They also encourage Presidents to attempt more than they can accomplish in any term of office. Thus, false expectations invite Presidents to overpromise and overextend themselves. This, in turn, creates the need for image-making activities. Such activities, in some cases, become the major task or work function of an administration. Soon, the emphasis, out of necessity, becomes style over substance. "The public-relations apparatus," as Cronin argues, "not only has directly enlarged the

Presidential work force but has expanded public-relations expectations about the Presidency at the same time. More disquieting is the fact that, by its very nature, this type of press-agentry, feeds on itself, and the resulting distortions encourage an ever increasing subordination of substance to style."[62]

The net result of this "cycle" is what Political Scientists refer to as "the paradoxical nature of the American Presidency." While nearly all Presidential scholars are quick to recognize the various paradoxes, few attempt to understand the "process" of their development. Simply stated, the public's expectations and demands of the Presidency invite paradoxical, two-faced behavior. As a President attempts to please "everyone," his behaviors are often contradictory and even "schizophrenic." As a President attempts to meet the diverse expectations of the citizenry, he is clearly placed in "no-win" situations.

There are ten rather distinguishable paradoxes of the American Presidency.[63] In terms of leadership, we desire a President to be moral and decent, yet in a time of crisis we demand forceful and decisive action. If the situation demands it, the nation will immediately applaud toughness and even ruthlessness. Gerald Ford was openly perceived to be a "nice guy" and "too decent" for Presidential responsibilities. However, Ford's decisive action in the *Mayaquez* rescue mission resulted in an eleven point gain in popularity and added esteem for his "tough response." Jimmy Carter received continual criticism for not being tough enough with the Iranians and Russians. Yet, the nation equally expected the lives of the American hostages in Iran to be preserved. Although a rescue attempt failed, resulting in eights American deaths, the immediate response was largely favorable. The "no-win" situation is clear. Does one attempt to preserve the lives of hostages and appear "weak" or attempt military action which risks the lives of the hostages and appear "strong." "We, in effect, demand the *sinsiter* as well as the *sincere,* President *mean* and President *nice*—tough and hard enough to stand up to a Khrushchev or to press the nuclear button; compassionate enough to care for the ill-fed, ill-clad, ill-housed."[64]

Also related to leadership, the President is required to be both programmatic as well as pragmatic. Presidents are elected, theoretically, based upon proposed programs; yet, once in office, we expect the President to be flexible and open to changing demands. As a nation there is little tolerance for rigidity or fuzziness. The most comfortable position, therefore, appears to be on the fence. The trick is to be specific but not too specific. Campaigns are exercises in winning an election and not in adult education.

More recently, a major theme of Presidential campaigns is "innovative leadership." Candidates are expected to have future visions, plans, and goals for the nation. Yet, a responsive Presidency is demanded which fulfills majority wishes. But should public opinion become the chief guide for leadership in America? To solve this dilemma, a President must show that indeed the architectural plans of the future are desired by the majority. This is achieved through persuasion utilizing various means.

Interestingly related to the above point, Americans seem to enjoy inspirational, "grand" rhetoric but are indeed becoming more suspect of "pie in the sky" solutions. Programs such as the "New Deal," "New Frontier," and "Great Society" raised hopes and optimism about the course of the nation as well as the future. But, as already argued, as promises have more frequently failed, the public's outrage increases—until another election year.

Increasingly, we want an open, cooperative, and sharing President while also applauding courageous, daring, and independent Presidential behavior. As a nation, secrecy is deplored yet some of the best "actions" this nation has every undertaken were shielded with secrecy. But more importantly, "the great Presidents have been the strong Presidents, who stretched their legal authority, who occasionally relied on the convenience of secrecy, and who dominated the other branches of government."[65]

One of the most interesting paradoxes of the office is the desire of most Americans for the President to be "non-political" and to make "non-partisan" decisions. Yet, in order to be elected and re-elected, a President must be a skillful politician. While being "above politics," he must also function as head of his party and cultivator of political sanctions. The chief executive, unlike many, functions as a Monarch, Prime Minister, and party head. Each of these, at certain times, creates advantages for certain groups at the expense of others.

Equally as interesting is the distinction between what it takes to become President and what is required to govern the nation. A good campaigner may not be a good administrator. Running for President requires ambiguity, style, and image. Governing requires mechanistic, concrete, and workable solutions. "Filling in the blanks" is often more difficult than providing the rationale. Jimmy Carter, in 1976, ran an almost perfect campaign. The image and issues espoused hit a very responsive note among the people. Once elected, however, he encountered an unresponsive bureaucracy and uncooperative Congress. As a result, the passage of "innovative" programs plus routine oversight of national concerns were indeed difficult. As the election year of 1980 approached, Carter's critics became more vocal about his lack of managerial capabilities. Indeed, the nation denied Carter a second term.

Historically, the longer a President is in office, the less public support he enjoys. It is rather ironic that as a President becomes better acquainted with the job, support diminishes. In terms of the Presidency, "familiarity breeds contempt."

Part of the broad American dream is the belief that any citizen may become President of the United States. We prize the notion of a "common man," one of "us" leading his fellowmen. Yet, once elected, we demand uncommon leadership, great insight, and vast knowledge from our Presidents. Carter wore many "hats" during the 1976 campaign. He was merely a "peanut farmer," "businessman," or "nuclear engineer" depending upon the audience. Politicians are fond of stating that "common sense needs to be returned to government." But simple solutions to major problems will not be tolerated by the public.

Finally, perhaps the greatest paradox of the office is in relation to its perceived power. Depending upon specific individuals and situations, the Presidency is either always too powerful or not powerful enough. The President should "take care of" something or "keep out" of an affair. The President, in one situation, should take all measures necessary to control inflation yet should not interfere with wages or prices of goods. As a nation we are quick to call for decisive action and equally as quick to yell "foul." More will be stated about the nature of Presidential power in the next section of this chapter.

How does one cope with paradox? The first step, of course, is recognition of the paradox. But to cope effectively one must go beyond recognition to understanding. This involves understanding the development and perpetuation of the paradoxes. Finally comes "appreciative" acceptance. As Cronin recommends to Presidents, "there are some excruciating no-win kind of contradictions in the job, and that one has to be a juggler and a balancer, and one has to have a thick skin to put up with the fact that you're damned if you do and damned if you don't — constantly."[66]

Summation

The American Presidency is a center of ever-accumulating functions, roles, obligations, and expectations. It is a universe unto itself that is constantly growing and expanding. From a distance one only notices singular "planets." But closer observation reveals a strong interdependence of the "planets." As an individual "interacts" with the "constitutionality" of the office, roles develop. These roles not only constrain individual behavior but also help create expectations of specified behavior. As expectations grow so does the job. The public's perceptions of the office are institutionalized into models, myths, history, and textbooks. Unrealistic demands and expectations produce reliance upon style over substance; image over issues. A President must appear active, moral, fair, intelligent, common, etc. But "appearances" are deceiving and paradoxical. For how can one be both active and passive, "common" and "uncommon," impotent and powerful? Such ambiguity demands a strategy. A strategy, however, is of little use unless there is a game to be played, however serious the game may be. But every game ultimately has rules. As Machiavelli declared many years ago:

> Those princes who have accomplished great things are the ones who had cared little for keeping promises and who knew how to manipulate the minds of men with shrewdness; ... he should appear, when seen and heard, to be all compassion, all faithfulness, all integrity, all kindness, all religion ... nothing makes a prince more esteemed than great enterprises and evidence of his unusual abilities ... take care not to infuriate the nobles, and to satisfy the common people and keep them happy; for this is one of the most important functions a prince has.[67]

The dynamic nature of the institution may now be appreciated. Yet the power of the analytic microscope should be increased. The task remains to investigate how Presidential roles are created, sustained, and permeated in society. In addition, the impact of the office upon the office holder remains to be investigated. For that alone is another "universe" complete with numerous "planets."

Roles Created, Permeated, and Sustained

Political roles, although undergoing constant modification, exist prior to any political event. Politicians, however, do not consciously decide each morning during what parts of the day they will act as a statesman, an administrator, or a partisan vote-getter. Yet, as already argued, public expectations of behavior and performance are rather clearly defined. Such expectations develop over time and consequently are slow in changing. Because political roles are fairly well defined, they are learned by politicians through the process of socialization. New legislators soon learn what roles are appropriate in various situations.

Roletaking, as Edelman notes, is action.[68] It is both behavioral and observable. The process or roletaking by politicians directly influences the behaviors of office holders by revealing public expectations and hence expected behavior. Edelman succinctly explains the process as follows:

> Through taking the roles of publics whose support they need, public officials achieve and maintain their positions of leadership. The official who correctly gauges the response of publics to his acts, speeches, and gestures makes those behaviors significant symbols, evoking common meanings for his audience and for himself and so shaping his further actions as to reassure his public and in this sense "represent" them.[69]

This process of role socialization, argues Rose, is "emotionally intense and highly compressed in time; it is the chief means by which people fit and are fitted into place in established institutions."[70]

One of the major points made in discussing the paradoxical nature of the Presidency, is that the expectations and functions of the office are often competing, conflicting, and contradictory. Role conflicts are an essential element in political life. Role conflict occurs "when contradictory types of behavior are expected from a person who holds different positions or when contradictory types of behavior are expected within one role."[71] A successful politician, therefore, is one who can handle role conflicts. Unfortunately, depending upon one's view, when a discrepancy develops between individual preferences and institutional role expectations, it is more often the individual that changes. For Richard Rose, the best measure of a politician's greatness is his ability to create new roles for an established office.[72] In fact, Rose views such an ability as one attribute of charismatic leadership.

There are, in fact, several categories of behavior "that can be utilized to lessen psychological stress resulting from role conflict."[73] They include: separating roles in time or space, placing priority on one role, merging conflicting roles into a single new compromise role, removing oneself from the situation, directing attention only toward the role being enacted, and changing beliefs so that the roles appear compatible or giving one role higher priority. Role redefinition, a ploy suggested by Rose, is perhaps the most difficult to achieve. To succeed, an individual must alter behavior but also attack the current value system in relation to the office plus persuade others to drop prior expectations. This is a most difficult task. For the politician, therefore, "the ability to learn new roles and shed old ones, thus effectively changing modes of behavior if not goals, is a prime requisite for a highly ambitious politician."[74]

Any discussion of political roles ultimately leads to a discussion of power. However, the treatment of that concept in this section differs greatly from traditional approaches to the concept. For the interactionist, power is not a concrete entity. Rather, it is a consequence, result, or product of many factors and processes. Likewise, the Presidency is greater than the sum of its parts. The nature of the office is more than the arithmetical total of all its functions. The Presidency is a focus of feelings and exists solely in the minds of men. As Barber argues, "the White House is not the President any more than the flag is the nation."[75] The Presidency is merely a collage of images, hopes, habits, and intentions shared by the nation who legitimizes the office and reacts to its occupants. Politically, most Americans know little about the workings of Congress or the Supreme Court. But in terms of the Presidency, the American people "respond" rather than simply "react" to the office. The President is the one symbolic figure upon which rests the hope for the nation's future.

This section will attempt to trace the development of our "intense" feelings for the Presidency. In doing so, we will see how roles are created, defined, and perpetuated through communication. The "processual" nature of Presidential power will also be investigated. But before such investigations begin, it is useful to contemplate briefly, from an interactionist perspective, our "political selves."

National political behavior, despite countless empirical studies, is really quite confusing upon analysis. As Kariel ponders, "if we are so mature, why are we so retarded? If we are so rich, why are we so poor? If we are so free, why are we so compliant? If we are so resourceful, why are we so clumsy?"[76] Political behavior tends to support clouded distinctions and moderated extremes. As a nation, citizens tend to reward those of ambiguities and punish those with concrete conclusions. Yet, roles are played and choices are made. The democratic myth dictates a renunciation of private interests in favor of majority benefits. But Abraham Maslow began a long march in questioning such a "reality." Politics provides, at the very least, enriching experiences and identifications. To participate in politics recognizes a sharing in the successes and a linkage to espoused values however "unreal" they may be.

Politics is primarily symbolic activity which touches the lives of a significantly large number of people.[77] Such activity has a unique and often profound meaning because, in the words of Kenneth Burke, man is uniquely "the symbol-using, symbol-making, and symbol-misusing animal."[78] Political reality, whose implications and consequences are felt and observable, is conveyed through the creation of "significant symbols."[79] Images of politics are largely, therefore, symbolic. The degree to which images of politics are useful and gratifying, according to Nimmo, is related to three factors:

> First, no matter how correct or incorrect, complete or incomplete may be one's knowledge about politics, it gives that person some way of understanding specific political events.... Second, the general likes and dislikes in a person's political images offer a basis for evaluating political objects.... Third, a person's self-image provides a way of relating one's self to others.[80]

Political images, then, are beneficial in an individual's evaluating and identifying with various political leaders, events, ideas, or causes. To understand the creation of Presidential roles within the context of public expectations and demands, childhood political socialization must be investigated.

Presidential Roles Created

Many attitudes about the Presidency stem from messages received in childhood about the virtues of various Presidents. Studies continually find that the President is ordinarily the first public official to come to the attention of young children.[81] David Easton and Robert Hess, in the late

1950's and early 1960's, surveyed over twelve thousand school children to study political socialization.[82] They found that up to ages 9 or 10, most children have difficulty in separating God and country. Extremely positive feelings are expressed toward the political system, especially the President, the policeman, the flag and the concept of freedom. Generally, by the age of nine, virtually every American child has some detailed awareness of the Presidency and can identify the incumbent President. Such cognizance of the American President, accoring to Greenstein, goes beyond national boundaries. He reports that surveys of children in Austria and Canada reveal that the name of the United States President is better known than the name of the Prime Ministers of their own countries.[83]

Long before children are informed about the specific functions of the Presidency, they view individual Presidents as exceptionally important and benign. Easton and Hess found that children stressed personal characteristics of the President which include: honesty, wisdom, helpfulness, powerful, good, and benign.[84] Such attitudes probably result from parents omitting negative aspects of the political world from the children plus the general tendency of children to perceive selectively more supportive characteristics of individuals in a wider environment. Even in 1973 at the height of the Watergate episode, Greenstein found "numerous idealized references to the President."[85] Thus, esteem and respect for the office independent of the occupant is established at an early age.

Within the literature, there are three general theories which attempt to explain why and how youth possess such positive and supportive feelings toward the Presidency.[86] Here, they may serve as a summation. Psychoanalytic theory argues that the bond between a parent and child generalizes to a feeling of warmth and admiration to anyone in authority positions. The greater the bond between parent and child, the greater the respect of authority figures. Developmental theory argues that children progress from simplistic understanding to increased cognitive awareness of the office. Young children do not possess the concepts or frames of reference required to understand but the most simple political communications. Consequently, the more positive elements, when shared, are retained. Some scholars argue that the positive feelings of political leaders by the nation's youth is simply a result of "sugarcoating of the political pill." Adults shield negative information about the harsh realities of the political world. Hence, political attitudes are first created in a vacuum of only positive orientations.

Presidential Roles Permeated

What is the relevance of the above for the American political system? Such orientations to the Presidency in adolescence have a profound influence on later attitudes. When political assessments of adult life conflict with earlier childhood attitudes, psychchologists argue that the longest held attitudes would most likely dictate the responses given.[87] Thus, even though adults are aware of the faults of the political systems, they continue to respect the Presidency above all other institutions.

Every year since World War II seven or eight of the ten most admired men and women are involved in national politics. And the President, regardless of performances, is among them.[88] Doris Graber, in a study designed to analyze images of Presidential candidates in the press during campaigns, found that citizens tend to extract selectively information about a President's personal image that is beyond the media content which ignores issue elements.[89] Therefore, apparently, citizens perceive and evaluate a President as a person rather than his policies and skill in office. According to Greenstein, when people are asked to indicate what they like or dislike about a President, they usually cite aspects of personal image.[90]

Another result of childhood socialization is the heavy dependency for leadership on the Presidency, especially in times of national crisis. Pious argues that in times of national emergency, we discard skepticism and return to childhood images of the Presidency.[91] As adults, we still desire to see the President as a combination of Washington and Lincoln, making wise decisions and working harder than the average citizen to preserve the quality of life.

A Presidential campaign emphasizes the childhood visions and qualities of the office. Hence, campaigns themselves perpetuate the "mythic" and heroic role demands of the office. To mobilize a nation is indeed a somewhat "mysterious" process. For McConnell it is the essential dimension of the Presidency resulting from becoming a "national symbol" and in so doing, give substance and purpose to the nation itself.[92] The process of selecting a President is important and vital. Campaigns may best be characterized as noisy, disorderly, contentious, and even absurd. "The gap between the indignity of the process and the grandeur of the end is enormous."[93] Yet, the process allows the opportunity of assessing and projecting Presidential qualities upon the candidates.

Media advisors must project appropriate images of the candidates which are always simplified depictions of reality. In a memo to Richard Nixon, Ray Price argued, "It's not what's there that counts, it's what is projected—and carrying it one step further, it's not what he projects but rather what the voter receives."[94] James Wooten, in addressing the 1976 Carter campaign, wrote that Carter "...believed that the candidate who took clear positions on every issue was not long for the political world. There would be only one issue on which a successful candidate would be judged that year, the amorphous, ethereal concept of integrity, honesty, trustworthiness, credibility."[95] Patrick Cadell is quoted as warning Carter during the transition that "too many good people have been beaten because they tried to substitute substance for style."[96] Is this ethically, logically, or even morally right? Carter's pollster Gerald Rafshoon believed that there was nothing wrong with a candidate adjusting himself to an ideology or "rhetorical stance" judged to be acceptable by the voters. Rafshoon argued to Wooten, "He was always Jimmy Carter...Hell, you wouldn't expect Sears Roebuck to step into a big multimillion dollar promotion without having the benefit of consumer research on what people are most interested in purchasing."[97] Consequently, the image projected by a candidate should meet the expectations and childhood "visions" of Presidential behavior. The best image is one that is vague enough for the voters to complete. In the simplest terms, this means that "conservatives" should be able to see the candidate as "conservative" and, likewise, "liberals" should be able to see the candidate as "liberal." Above all, this should be done without seeming contradictory or insincere.

From this perspective an election is seen not simply as a reflection of the preference for one individual over another. Rather, it is a composite of all the individual desires, hopes, frustrations, and anger of citizens encompassing an infinite number of issues or concerns. However chaotic, the process has value. As McConnell notes:

> Purists may well wish for more graceful campaigning, and more incisive and intellectually elevated debates. Quite possibly, however, achieving these desirable conditions might rob the process of much of its vitality and leave the ultimate winner with no accurate sense of the temper of the American people. A Presidential election is, above all, an articulation of the mood of the electorate.[98]

By inauguration day a candidate has emerged as President. A tremendous transformation, at least in the eyes of the public, has occurred. Americans want and even need to believe that the common man they elevated to the Presidency is a "Lincolnesque" bearer of infinite wisdom and benevolence. The perceived qualities are confirmed as soon as the candidate takes the oath of office. This phenomenon is beautifully described by William Mullen:

> A mysterious process begins to take place as soon as it is clear that one of the aspirants to the office has been elected. His defeated opponent writes his congratulations, promises support, and wishes the President-elect every success. The press points to fresh opportunities and the dawning of a new era. Polls conducted after the election find far more people saying they voted for the victorious nominee than the ballots indicate actually did. Many of those who voted against the man as a candidate begin to view him in a different light. Support increases among the population at large as the magic of the office begins to lead its coloration to the next executive. By inauguration day, a large majority will say they support the President, regardless of how slim his electoral margin may have been.[99]

The public's relationship with the Presidency is more than a search for the fulfillment of childhood notions of the office. For some time empirical and clinical evidence has shown that the office provides, for a large portion of the population, an outlet for expression of deep, often unconscious personality needs and conflicts. Harold Lasswell, as early as 1930 in his classic *Psychopathology and Politics*, argued that private needs become displaced onto public objects and rationalized in terms of general political principles.[100] Greenstein, a student of Lasswell, continually investigated this phenomena in relation to the Presidency.[101] He recognizes six major psychological uses of the Presidency for the population.

1. The office serves as a cognitive aid by providing a vehicle for the public becoming aware of the functions, impact, and politics of government.

2. The Presidency provides an outlet for affect, feelings, and emotions. The office serves as a focal point of pride, despair, hope, as well as frustration. It can easily be responsible, in the eyes of the public, for all that is "bad" or for all that is "good."

3. The office serves as a means of vicarious participation. The President becomes an object of identification and consequently Presidential efforts become citizen efforts resulting in a sharing of heightened feelings of potency.

4. Especially in times of crisis or uncertainty, the Presidency functions as a symbol of national unity. When a President acts, it is the nation acting as one voice expressing one sentiment.

5. Likewise, the office serves as a symbol of stability and predictability. We assume that the President is knowledgeable and in control of events thus minimizing danger or surprise.

6. Finally, the Presidency serves as a "lightning rod" or object of displacement. The office is the ultimate receptacle for personal, which becomes national, feelings and attitudes. The President becomes either idealized or the ultimate scapegoat. Truman's cliche, "The buck stops here" is true—at least in the minds of the public.

Presidential Roles Sustained

How does the Presidency of today differ from that of George Washington? Most scholars would reply that the office today is much more powerful. It directly affects every citizen, for the President is responsible for setting national policy and goals. In this complex world, nearly every

Presidential decision affects all citizens economically and psychologically. The office, if not the office holder, enjoys a kind of world wide prestige unknown in the days of George Washington. Rossiter asserts "that the outstanding feature of American constitutional development has been the growth of the power and prestige of the Presidency."[102] The powers of the American Presidency, both constitutionally and pragmatically, have been a subject of endless fascination and study to American political scientists. As noted earlier in this chapter, the catalogue of Presidential functions and duties now encompasses several volumes. Yet, the more that Presidential power is studied and analyzed, the more abusive it becomes. The formal powers granted in the Constitution are indeed negligible and Congress has even challenged these.

Perhaps the greatest difficulty in understanding Presidential power is the misconception that the exercise of power is the consequence of "rational" decision making. The task, therefore, becomes simply one of identifying all the participants and influences that go into the process of decision making. The illusion which results from such an approach tends to view decisions as choices among clearly understood alternatives made by knowledgeable actors. However, close examination of key historical Presidential decisions tends to reveal a process earmarked by luck, accident, and general lack of information. The Cuban Missile Crisis is a prime example.[103] At the very least, the President should not be viewed as a "genralissimo" issuing a never ending series of commands and having them immediately obeyed.

Prior works mentioning Presidential power usually emphasize one of three approaches.[104] A historical approach to Presidential power views power as a consequence of individual Presidents attempting to maximize their personal orientation to the office. Historians focus on individual influence, control of the country's destiny, and the President's capacity to draw talented men to his administration. Electoral results, partisan politics, and mobilization of public opinion are key elements in studying Presidential power.

Many political scientists prefer to focus on the formal powers of the office. Presidential power is a direct result of constitutional authority, Congressional authority, and the system of checks and balances. Individual Presidents are judged on the "quantity" of power exhibited ranging from crisis to crisis and administration to administration. Such an approach serves as an alarm system to Presidential abuse of power and authority.

Within recent years, psychological orientations to power focus on leadership and personality factors. The concern here is on the characteristics that enable a President to persuade and influence Congress as well as the nation.

In the past, little attention has been given to the social scientific study of Presidential power. The above approaches primarily focus on the

of this section has been to focus on the *processes* of power and not to provide a systematic treatment of the subject. For the interactionist, power is a "quality" of interaction and not an entity.

As already noted in this chapter, power in early works, was based upon the constitutional roles or functions performed by the President. Each "job" carried unique authority. Rossiter, by recognizing five additional "extra-constitutional" roles of the President, effectively argued that Presidential power had indeed expanded with the job. Again, the major idea was that each role was a source of power. Yet, most of the early books emphasized the system of "checks and balances" which controlled Presidential power. Rossiter was quick to identify ten elements that limit the power of the President which include: a four year term, no third term, Congress ability to override the veto, frequent reports to Congress, various limits on power of appointments, Supreme Court decisions, various Congressional authority, the federal administration and bureaucracy, the opposition political party, and simply world opinion.[105] But even Rossiter recognized that Presidential power was more than simple "actions." For Presidential power "operates within a grand and durable pattern of private liberty and public morality, which means that it operates successfully only when the President honors the pattern by selecting ends and means that are characteristically American."[106]

Neustadt's classic, *Presidential Power,* was the first major work which emphasized the importance and role individual Presidents had in developing power and influence.[107] His goal was to show how a President can become a powerful leader and what a President must do if he hopes to maintain influence over others. Neustadt believed "that the Presidency as an office is so weak that the President as a person has to watch every single choice he makes today, with particular concern for its effect on his prospective influence tomorrow."[108]

Presidential leadership, for Neustadt, "is not so much his own actions but his influence on the actions of others. Not what he does, but what he gets done, indicates his true powers."[109] Realistically, then, "Presidential power is the power to persuade" and consequently is not guaranteed to any President. A President must, first, want to maximize his power and second, be willing to bargain and trade "advantages."

A President's influence or power, according to Neustadt, comes from three sources. The first is from the bargaining advantages he has resulting from the office. Second, a great deal of influence comes from a President's professional reputation comprised of his willingness to use sanctions at his disposal. Finally, the public prestige of a President allows even greater latitude in expanding and developing influence. Ultimately, the interaction of the four variables of personality, experience, events and conditions, and vantage points determines a President's actual power.

Neustadt's scheme is both content and value free. There is a heavy reliance upon Presidential choices. Thus, the emphasis is still on concrete decisions and choices made by a President which fails to appreciate the nature of power from an interactionist perspective. Perhaps the closest analysis of Presidential power which more fully recognizes its "dynamic" "processual" nature is rendered in a forthcoming work by Myron Hale. Hale distinguishes among Presidential influence, authority, and power. Such a distinction is necessary, according to Hale, "in order not only to improve our understanding of Presidential politics, but to evaluate Presidential power and policy results."[111] For Hale, "Presidential influence" is the encompassing term which is rooted in Presidential authority. Institutional authority is founded upon the office as defined in the constitution plus the status and prestige associated with the office. Personal authority is the development and maintenance of individual credibility. Importantly, institutional authority is transferable, personal authority is not. In addition, the authority of a President, in either category, depends upon the acceptance of such authority as appropriate and legitimate. "If the President's behavior does not meet the normative expectations of the society, he may lose legitimacy. If the President loses legitimacy, authority will vanish, and with it political power."[112]

Hale's treatment of Presidential power has several advantages. First it emphasizes the dynamic, process nature of power rather than results or end products of power. Second, the approach recognizes the importance of interaction of the people with the office and the office with the people in the development of power. Third, Hale clearly distinguishes between the "power" of the office and the "power" of the office holder. Finally, the model acknowledges the importance of public expectations in assessing Presidential power.

The Perceptual, Relational, and Interactive Nature of Power

Power is a relational phenomenon and not principally a psychological one. Power is created and exists resulting from social relationships. Individuals may possess unique strengths, knowledge or skills, but these capabilities in no way constitute social power. Of course, one's personal characteristics can enhance power in a particular situation. The simple point is that power is something people participate in rather than something people react to.

There is a tremendous difference between, as recognized by Koenig, an imagined Presidency and the Presidency of reality.[113] The imagined Presi-

available in any situation. "The imagined Presidency is a euphoric impression of its past, present, and future, and is grounded partly in reality and partly in fancy. It exaggerates the office's strength, encouraged by the substantial power it actually possesses, the prestige built in its past and the pomp that surrounds it."[114] Yet, perceptions often mean more than actual power or force. In the international climate, the perception of a leader's resolve can have a greater impact on the number of a nation's aircraft carriers. Hugh Sidey notes, in reference to the Iranian hostage situation, that "terrorist tactics can mock stockpiled nukes."[115] "The winning of the President's power," according to Theodore White, "lies in noise and clangor, the flogging of the emotions and the appeal to all the tribal pasts of America."[116]

The Presidency simply is not as "powerful" as many citizens believe. An aid to President Truman is quoted as saying,

> The most startling thing a new President discovers is that his world is *not* monolithic. In the world of the Presidency, giving an order does not end the matter. You can pound your fist on the table or you can get mad or you can blow it all and go out to the golf course. But nothing gets done except by endless follow-up, endless kissing and coaxing, endless threatening and compelling.[117]

Richard Cheney, an advisor to several contemporary Presidents concurs by stating that "there's a tendency for us to think, gee, the President has enormous power, that the people around him are powerful people, that they sit around all day and they wield something called power. Well, when you get there you quickly find that's not the case."[118]

From this discussion, the first important point to be made is that the perception of power implies an expectation of power. "Every expectation" argues McConnell, "proclaims that he is a man of power, and at every point the expectation is itself a source of power."[119] Second, power is not simply a quality that a person possesses like brown hair and blue eyes. Rather, it is a relational phenomenon depending upon citizen perceptions, history of the office, and personal development of mass perceptions of the power of the office.

For Pious, Presidential choices serve as the basis for Presidential power. A President's use of his constitutional prerogatives sets the stage for Congressional action and judicial interpretations. His "theory" of Presidential power specifies that one should "concentrate on the constitutional authority that the President asserts unilaterally through various rules of constitutional construction and interpretation, in order to resolve crises or important issues facing the nation."[120] Such a theory, however, still lacks the dynamic personal development of "power." There is a confusion between substance of power and style of power. As McConnell observes, "while the appearance of power is sometimes mistaken for the substance of power, appearance can occasionally be a useful substitute for reality and indeed may even become reality."[121] Different problems and skills involved in politics result in various Presidential "styles" of power. Woodrow Wilson and John Kennedy emphasized appearances of leadership and moral appeals to the nation. In contrast, Lyndon Johnson relied on personal contact and pressure on individual congressmen for impact. Bryce Harlow, advisor to several contemporary Presidents, recalls, "LBJ was the most forceful person in relationship to people that I have ever met or expect to meet. He could charm you, he could frighten you in an incredible variety of ways that came to him automatically."[122] The key, perhaps, is knowing and utilizing the appropriate "style" to the problems of the times. The use of an inappropriate "style" could easily result in being perceived as "weak," or "mean," or "compromising," etc.

Independent of "styles" is skill or the techniques used to develop "styles." In the words of Wildavsky, "to meet the constitutional duties of the office as well as the strong expectations of others, Presidents must persuade, bargain, or coerce."[123] President Truman's famous retort about the power of the Presidency is now classic among scholars: "...the principal power that the President has is to bring people in and try to persuade them to do what they ought to do without persuasion. That's what I spend most of my time doing. That's what the powers of the President amounts to."[124] For the symbolic interactionist, this is a key observation. Power, defined as the control of others, results from getting others to accept one's view and perspective of "reality." To do so, one must control, influence, and sustain one's own definition of the situation by "acting" which creates an image that ultimately leads others to behave voluntarily in the desired way. Persuasion involves awakening in an individual a voluntary inclination toward certain courses of action. The next chapter focuses on the role that situation plays in the public's view of the Presidency.

A President is required, to persuade successfully, to manipulate valued political symbols appropriate to political culture.[125] Values and beliefs are identified, emphasized, and utilized in shaping a reality upon which to act. As Peter Hall succinctly states:

> The politician is potentially always on stage. Every aspect of his behavior can become part of a public performance which must be managed and controlled to mobilize support. Many of his activities will be essentially symbolic, i.e., for the purpose of creating the desired identity in order to draw the audience into *his* drama.[126]

The notion of Presidential power is grounded in *perceptions* of power. Corresponding expectations are based on images of power created or "styles" that develop. But, essential to each of these steps of the process is interaction. Persuasion, bargaining, and coercion are all modes of interaction subject to various styles and approaches.

A Communication Model of Presidential Power

Authority-Influence Continuum

Myron Hale's distinction between authority and influence is very valuable.[127] In the realm of politics, the concepts, however, exist as a continuum. The ultimate authority for the Presidency is the American constitution which specifies rules and procedures for Presidential duties and behavior. Although rather specific, the constitution is subject to debate and varieties of interpretation. To define power simply as the effective use of authority is missing a tremendous point. If power is the "legitimate" use of authority, then what is "legitimate?" To Machiavelli, legitimate means to expand or increase power at all costs. Indeed, any "use" of power implies the personal, influence dimension. The "influence" aspect is the "how" to use power. Nicholas von Hoffman argues that "the more narrowly limited the power of the office, the more important the personality of the office-holder."[128] An individual is as "powerful" or "powerless" as they desire to be. Gordon Tullock concurs by arguing that *real power* is much more restricted than *apparent power.* "Real power is, by necessity, strictly limited, and its exercise requires hard and unremitting work. Apparent power on the other hand, can be substantially unlimited and can be more easily obtained."[129] But, of course, the perception of power with little or no legitimate authority to reinforce it is of little consequence. More importantly, the mere perception of power is dangerous. Olsen correctly observes that "social influence is an instance of power in which outcomes are not predetermined. Influence can only be attempted, not enforced, and its results are always problematic."[130]

In terms of the model, the first continuum is the authority-influence continuum (See figure 1). Authority refers to the laws, statues, or constitution which prescribe duties, responsibilities, and behaviors of the President.

Figure 1

AUTHORITY
(constitutional, legalistic, prescribed)

INFLUENCE
(interpersonal, bargaining skills, personality)

Such documents legitimizes one's actions. The structure of an organization is one method of clearly delineating relative power and authority. Obviously, an individual may utilize organizational roles and status as resources for enhancing personal power and prestige. A difficult question becomes: How do we tell whether a person is acting as a legitimate representative of an organization or acting as an independent agent attempting to increase or exercise interpersonal power and influence? Hence, the authority-influence dimension.

The influence element of the continuum refers to the overt attempts to increase relative power by relying on persuasive and bargaining skills and techniques. Other factors include public prestige and credibility.

Presidential leadership clearly involves aspects of both the elements of influence and authority. Extremes in either case may be fatal. Watergate continually decreased Nixon's influence without decreasing his authority. The result, however, was an ineffective Presidency. The secret is, perhaps, to reach a balance between the two extremes. Some scholars would argue that President Reagan found just the right niche in getting his tax cut proposal through Congress in July, 1981. Reagan prepared the necessary legislation, explaind the proposal in a national televised address, and defended the proposed tax plan at a subsequent press conference. But equally important, Reagan privately met and telephoned key members of Congress until the measure was voted upon.

Traditional views of political power are founded upon the notion that orders given by "the government" are legitimate because they are ultimately approved by the citizenry and are in accordance with the constitution. But the enforcement of various governmental orders relies upon the psychological skills and techniques of "coercion," not ideas of legitimacy.

Openness-Secrecy Continuum

Equal access to information is vital to the functioning of a democracy. American society has gone to great lengths to protect its citizens' access to information ranging from the Revolutionary Bill of Rights to the more recent Freedom of Information Act of 1967. Dissemination of knowledge is required to insure a well informed citizenry. Yet, within the realm of politics, information is indeed "power." Edelman observes that "political beliefs and perceptions are very largely not based upon empirical observations or indeed, upon 'information' at all."[131] People get information, change it, store it, pass it around, amplify it, and distort it. Political realities created may or may not be founded upon facts. Hence, information becomes a valuable commodity both at the national level as well as the interpersonal level. Perry London argues that "every kind of information and every medium for communicating it is potentially useful as an instrument of control."[132] For him, control by information includes nearly all of the communication and persuasion methods that our society has traditionally regarded as legitimate, ranging from propaganda to education.[133] Vital to persuasion is knowing how to use information that is relevant to another person's interests and goals.

For purposes of this model, the openness-secrecy continuum refers to the general use of information by a President as a method of control or inducing desired behavior (see Figure 2). The model recognizes that there exist a rather wide range of options between complete secrecy or complete disclosure of information which may be persuasively powerful. The control of information enhances one's problem-solving ability. Thus, this dimension refers to a President's general orientation to secrecy or openness in daily interaction.

Figure 2

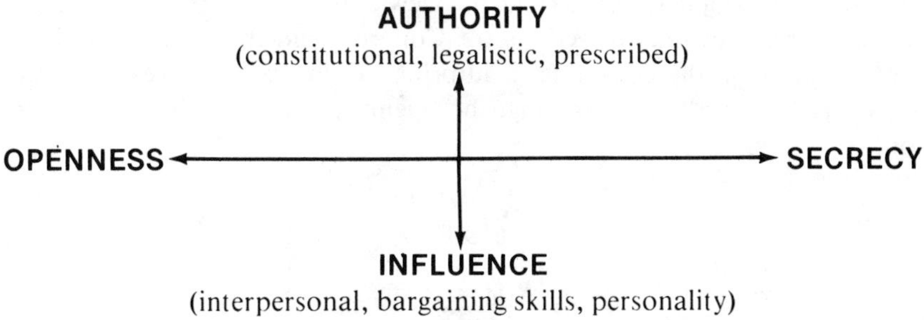

AUTHORITY
(constitutional, legalistic, prescribed)

OPENNESS ←————————————————→ **SECRECY**

INFLUENCE
(interpersonal, bargaining skills, personality)

Lyndon Johnson is most often cited as a President who frequently used secrecy as an instrument of control. Chester Cooper notes that Johnson's "compulsive secrecy was not so much a conscious conspiracy as it was a reflection of the President's personal style—a style that favored a "closed" rather than an 'open' system of policymaking."[134] Perhaps the real task for any President is to keep secrecy from becoming deception and honesty mere publicity. At either extreme the nation is subjected to coercion and not persuasion. This model, therefore, views information as a means of control and the degree or use of secrecy-openness is a characteristic technique of increasing or defining Presidential power.

Four Orientations to Power

With the two continuums intersecting, four orientations to Presidential power may be identified (see Figure 3).[135] Each quadrant possesses unique characteristics and heavy reliance upon any one of the orientations may be recognized as a President's "style" of power. Of course, Presidents use all four orientations; each of which has advantages in specific situations. The model is flexible, therefore, by allowing analysis of specific Presidential decisions and actions as well as in characterizing individual Presidential performances.

"Institutional"

Quadrant I of figure 3 represents the "institutional" orientation to power. In this mode, the President maximizes openness and legitimate authority. Power stems from the legal foundations of the institution. Questions of Presidential power are observable and consequently clearly "right or wrong," "good or bad." Thus, actions are based upon constitutional, legal authority. This orientation views the powers of the Presidency conservatively. The individual maintains a high belief in the rationality of the people. The President views his major role as one of management, providing directions for Congress and the public to follow. Jimmy Carter, at the beginning, held primarily this perspective. Throughout Carter's Presidential campaign he openly promised "I'll never lie to you."

Figure 3

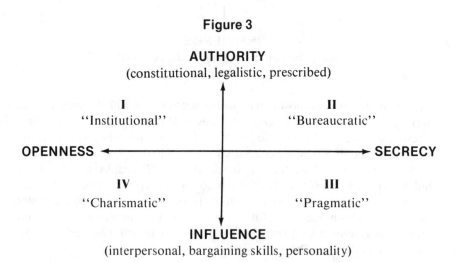

AUTHORITY
(constitutional, legalistic, prescribed)

| I | II |
| "Institutional" | "Bureaucratic" |

OPENNESS ←————————————————→ **SECRECY**

| IV | III |
| "Charismatic" | "Pragmatic" |

INFLUENCE
(interpersonal, bargaining skills, personality)

The limitations of this orientation are fairly obvious. There exists a lack of the ability to motivate and persuade the public and key individuals who surround the office. Indeed, Carter's failure to get his energy program passed by Congress is largely because of his failure to "wine and dine" key Congressional leaders. Carter perhaps naively believed that if he effectively recognized and articulated the problem, subsequent corrective action and behavior would naturally follow. In addition, if the powers of the Presidency are viewed conservatively, then available sanctions are limited as well. The "institutional" orientation to power simply ignores the dynamics of the office. It treats the power of the institution as strictly, empirically defined ignoring the emotional, symbolic significance of the office. The Presidency is more than a management office. To identify a problem, isolate the variables, and construct a solution is not the same as generating support, persuading a public of a law's necessity, and getting the legislation passed through Congress. Leadership, as a quality, differs from simple management. Because the office is "public", structure and legalistic formulations are of little consequence when attempting to gauge the "power" of the Presidency.

"Bureaucratic"

Quadrant II of figure 3 represents the "bureaucratic" orientation to power. Presidential actions are based on legitimate authority but generally surrounded by secrecy. The President has the authority to issue unilateral, nonreciprocal commands with government and fully expect them to be followed. What often results, however, is large scale bargaining among individuals positioned in the hierarchy of government. The key to this orientation to power is Presidential bargaining. The President has authority to take specified actions but prefers to avoid publicity. The President utilizes the "machinery" of government to obtain the implementation of certain policies. Lines of organizational authority and hierarchy are maximized. This kind of power is no longer ideological but merely psychological relying upon both physical and psychological force.

The goal here is not deception but efficiency and internal control. This orientation to power promotes operational efficiency through standardized administration thus ensuring internal control and coordination. During the Cuban Missile Crisis, President Kennedy relied heavily upon the bureaucratic orientation to power. There was never any doubt about his authority to handle the situation, but Kennedy severely limited the information concerning the negotiations of the crisis to both the American people as well as high ranking governmental officials. Even segments of the military were not fully informed when given commands of action.[136] Lyndon Johnson's secret ground war in Laos between 1963 and 1968 was also of this nature. But this orientation to power is not limited to crisis situations. The focus of the orientation, however, is upon efficiency and implementation. Laws and statutes may proclaim "equal opportunity employment" and non-discrimination but how are those laws implemented and enforced? The denying of effective political participation of blacks certainly occurred after the passage of the Voting Rights Act. An agreement, of course, is only as "good" as the people who sign it. Information is a tool used in the bargaining process. This orientation is very similar to Neustadt's model of Presidential power.[137] As already noted, he argued that the power to persuade lies in the ability to bargain. Abuse of Neustadt's model leads to a discussion of the "pragmatic" orientation to power.

"Pragmatic"

Quadrant III of figure 3 represents the true Machiavellian perspective of power. The President attempts to maximize power at all costs. There is a heavy reliance upon secrecy and interpersonal skills of persuasion and bargaining. Presidential requests, actions, and behaviors go beyond legitimate authority. This approach, however, is rational because decisions are based upon cost-benefit analyses. Considerations may include questions of national security, domestic political environment, opponent strengths, or simply desires to conceal incompetence, embarrassment, or governmental inefficiency. Secrecy easily becomes deception and influence a matter of coercion. Kennedy's assassination plots to eliminate Castro as well as Nixon's Watergate endeavors fall under this category. It should be emphasized that this orientation to power is not inherently bad; rather, it provides more opportunity for abuse. Power is a function of individual endeavors to maximize bargaining advantages including elements of public prestige.

"Charismatic"

Quadrant IV of figure 3 represents the "charismatic" orientation to power. The President's personality characteristics are key to his persuasive efforts. Information is not used as a weapon or bargaining tool. The individual has an attraction, affectivity, and identification that is most appealing and persuasive. Key interpersonal skills developed include the abilities to: create a sense of obligation and loyalty with individuals with whom the President interacts, foster unconscious identification with subordinates or ideas they profess, and create perceptions of dependence with those with whom he interacts. While Jimmy Carter avoided this orientation until the latter part of his Presidency, Ronald Reagan is more successful in utilizing this style.

Summation

Power consists of potential (resources), action (behavior), and patterns of interaction (style). Power is a relative measure of an individual's potential to get others to do what the person wants them to do. Power-oriented behavior consists of actions taken by an individual whose purpose is to obtain, maintain, or increase his relative power.[138] A person's style or orientation to power consists of identifiable patterns of interactions involving the elements of information, position, and interpersonal skills.

The somewhat speculative and conceptual model presented here provides a framework for analyzing the dynamics of power rather than simply the resources of power. Money is power only when it is spent. But *how* the money is spent reveals an orientation or style of power. The point may best be illustrted by using the characters from the popular television show "Dallas." Both money and information are valuable resources of power for J.R. Ewing. Clearly J.R. has a unique style or orientation toward obtaining, maintaining and increasing power which differs greatly from his brother Bobby Ewing. Although both have nearly equal resources and interpersonal skills, J.R. prefers secrecy and covert manipulation whereas Bobby prefers openness and legitimate persuasion. Thus, J.R.'s styles are more "bureaucratic" and "pragmatic"; Bobby's styles are more "charismatic" and "institutional." At the very least, the model forces the scholar to recognize the importance of interaction when discussing the phenomenon of power in human society.

Adpatation of "Self" to the Presidency

Any discussion of expectations which surround the Presidency leads to the consideration of how individual occupants of the office fit into the already established and defined role. But, as nearly all scholars recognize, there is no apprenticeship or training an individual may obtain in preparation for the Presidency. There is no convenient book or guide which provides a detailed step by step analysis of the requirements and demands of the office. As Theodore White observes, the office is "defined not so much by law as by the nature of men and the pressures of history."[139] Thus, what separates a good President from one not so good is the ability to "perceive" the office and "become" President. The purpose of this section is to view the impact of the office upon the office holder and more importantly, to observe the process of "becoming" President of the United States.

The self, as defined in chapter two, is a social object that one shares with others in interaction. It comprises the individual's view of himself in all the various statuses and roles which dictate one's behavior toward all of the objects of one's experience. A "political self," then, refers to an individual's view of oneself in the single-role of political actor or one's package of orientations regarding politics. One's self is isolated, interpreted, and defined socially. An individual's perception of the political role consists of all norms established socially resulting from interaction. One's political self becomes a separate object for investigation. As an object, the self can be modified, evaluated, and reinforced. The political self, as a process, involves continual mediation between one's own impulses and the expectations of others. A political self arises from political socialization. Political socialization, as noted earlier, is a process of adopting and adapting the self to the actions of others through roletaking.

Political learning may be characterized as interpersonal, accumulative, and adaptive.[140] As interpersonal, it requires recognizing, evaluating, and defining self from the perspectives of others. As accumulative, political learning occurs in stages (i.e., pretending and imitating). Political learning is adaptive resulting from the capacity to change self depending on political environment, beliefs, values, and expectations.

The Presidency is certainly a grand office. The civil service job classification is Executive I. In addition to a salary of $200,000 and $50,000 for expenses, the office holders have Air Force One, twelve Boeing 707's, eight VH-3 helicopters, and specially constructed Lincoln Continentals at their disposal. The White House grounds have thirty gardeners who maintain the outside but more than that number who maintain the house itself. The President also has access to Camp David which is run by 150 Naval personnel. Can such a job not have a profound impact upon the individual occupant? Presidential advisor Richard Cheney thinks not:

> I can't think of a recent time when a man became President and didn't have it have some kind of impact on his ego. You know, all of a sudden there are hundreds of people willing to wait on you hand and foot and do whatever needs to be done. Helicopters, Air Force One, Limousines, Secret Service Agents, cheering multitudes and 'Hail to the Chief' — you'd have to be less than human not to respond to those kinds of trappings that go with the office. And it does, I think, affect people.[141]

Most recent scholars are quick to recognize that the office has a tremendous impact upon the occupant. As President, one becomes enobled despite past failures or preparation for the job. Presidents become captives of campaign illusions of self grandeur. According to Reedy, "a President would have to be a dull clod indeed to regard himself without a feeling of awe. The atmosphere of the White House is calculated to instill in any man a sense of destiny."[142] The President walks where Jefferson walked, sleeps where Lincoln slept, writes on Wilson's desk, and dines where the Roosevelts dined. The President becomes the personification of the people. "The President becomes the nation," as Reedy observes, "and when he is insulted, the nation is insulted; when he has a dream, the nation has a dream; when he has an antagonist, the nation has an antagonist."[143]

Thus, the environment of the Presidency is one of adulation, respect, awe, and "divine." When such an environment affects the individual, it also affects job performance. Most alarming, for Reedy, is that "virtually all the information he received was presented by people who desired to ·

retain his favor."[144] The central question becomes, therefore, "What can a President do to resist the idolatry and respect for a national symbol?"

Scholars have been concerned with the impact of certain personalities upon the office. Perhaps the first person to systematically evaluate the impact of the office upon individuals was Bruce Buchanan.[145] In his recent work, Buchanan posits:

1. there is an essential, trans-historical Presidential experience, capable of influencing *any* incumbent, and
2. the origins of this common experience are essentially constitutional...over years sedimentary accretion of additional formal and informal functions and expectations for which the Presidency is now held accountable,
3. the experience of concern is essentially psychological: a four-fold "environmental press" created and sustained by the role requirements of the Presidency.

For Buchanan, the core or generic functions of the office include: symbol, policy advocate, mediator, and crisis manager. These four functions "virtually guarantees recurring and consistent kinds of personal exposures for the President" which "are the brute realities with which he must contend."[146] These exposures or pressures include: frustration, dissonance, deference, and stress. Such exposures, because the President is ego-involved, affect job performance as well as the individual psyche.

Stress results from the role requirements of mediator and crisis manager. These roles may be characterized as being unpredictale, physically wearing, and emotionally draining. Buchanan argues that the exposure to stress, which is chronic and intense, results in threats to self-concept, decline in performance and effectiveness, physical deterioration, psychological disorientation, and formalistic management system employment.

Deference results from the symbolic nature of the office. The majestic treatment of Presidents causes status inequality, inflation of self-concept, and distorted perception of external events. Such exposure manifests distortion of social comparison processes, "over identification" with the office, and misinformed decisions. A President easily incorporates the trappings, powers, and perogatives of the Presidency into one's self-definition. Every President is treated as if uniquely gifted and wise. In such a world, "reality" is very difficult to assess.

A President is exposed to dissonance mainly resulting from the policy advocate and symbolic functions of the job. Presidents are constantly pressured to misrepresent or distort themselves to various national constituencies. Such a continual pressure causes further misrepresentation, erosion of truth norms, and self-delusion. Consequently, lying and misrepresentation (i.e., as in Watergate, Gulf of Tonkin incident, etc.) become accepted practices.

The role of policy advocate, according to Buchanan, produces continual frustration. The impact of such exposure is revealed in increased preoccupation with personal success and survival as well as concern for prevailing over the opposition. Frustration manifests itself in threat of self-concept, arrogation of power (e.g., misuse of CIA and FBI), plebiscitary Presidency (e.g., discrediting Press and Congress) and provocation of confrontation (e.g., Roosevelt's staking the Supreme Court or Nixon's refusal to cooperate in Watergate proceedings).

The key to handling the exposures to stress, deference, dissonance, and frustration, according to Buchanan, is to have a good self-concept and high self-esteem. He posits that "Presidents lacking in self-esteem are more likely to display variants of the 'undesirable' behavior than Presidents possessed of high self-esteem."[147] I somewhat disagree with this conclusion. Most Presidents behave as President based on their own perceptions of Presidential behavior. If they perceive the office as all powerful, they will become all powerful. Each President confronts the "role" and must adapt to the office. This "transformation" is readily noticeable in Presidential memoirs and writings. One notices, first, a comparison process whereby the individual assesses his capabilities of *being* President. Next, one finds considerable speculation as to the awe when one *is* President. Finally, as a result of interacting with the public, historical expectations, and individual views of the office, the person *becomes* President.

Potential Presidents must at some point assume their perceived role of the Presidency. "When playing at being someone else," Hugh Duncan argues, "the self realizes its own nature at the same time it realizes the nature of the person whose role is being played."[148] Author Schlesinger recognized this phenomenon in John Kennedy. Schlesinger suggests that Kennedy's writing of *Profiles in Courage* aided in defining his "political self" and working out the continual dilemma of political means versus political ends.[149] Schlesinger writes:

> Gradually there evolved a sense of his own identity as a political man, compounded of his growing mastery of the political arts and, even more, of his growing understanding that, for better or worse, his public self had to be faithful to his private self.[150]

An integral part of this process is recognizing the public's expectations of the role. The eventual "Presidential self" includes all the subjective thoughts, feelings, and needs which are associated with the role. Naturally, therefore, Presidents consciously and unconsciously set the scenes to create preferred images in their interactions with others. As Schlesinger relates, "Every politican has to fake a little, and Kennedy was a politician determined to become President. He was prepared to do many things, to cut corners, to exploit people and situations, to 'go, go, go' even to merchandise himself."[151]

Perhaps the most profound recognition of the importance of establishing a "Presidential image" was that made by Lyndon Johnson upon the death of John Kennedy. Johnson realized that the first impression of his Presidency would be most critical. Although Johnson had been a senior Senator and Vice President, meetings with old acquaintances and political allies must reflect a "Presidential tone." Kearns writes:

> He knew they were looking at him afresh; he knew they would be thinking what he would have been thinking on seeing an old friend or an associate suddenly become President. The initial definition of the situation would provide the basis for all future meetings.[152]

A clear, systematic process of transformation from candidate to President appears in nearly every Presidential biography. Carter serves as a good example. The origins of Carter's decision to run for President are somewhat hard to pinpoint. According to Carter, it was a combination of conscious and subconscious reflection.

> I think it just evolved, probably without my being aware of it at all, until at some point or another I entertained the idea, probably for just a split second and probably without realizing I had, and then it probably occurred again, this time maybe for a little longer than the first, and also probably without my actual conscious realization that it was there, until finally when I acknowledge that it was there, I couldn't remember when it wasn't there.[153]

Carter speaks rather specifically about his assessing and comparing his qualities for the Presidency in 1975. In doing so, Carter became an object unto himself for evaluation and possibly adaptation.

> I have always looked on the Presidency of the United States with reverence and awe, and I still do. But recently I have begun to realize that the Presidency is just a human being. I can almost remember when I began to change my mind and form this opinion.... Then during 1971 and 1972 I met Richard Nixon, Spiro Agnew, George McGovern, Henry Jackson, Hubert Humphrey, Ed Muskie, George Wallace, Ronald Reagan, Nelson Rockefeller, and other Presidential hopefuls, and I lost my feeling of awe about Presidents.[154]

In relaying the same sentiments at a Press conference in Little Rock, he added, "I didn't feel inferior anymore. I feel that I am as qualified to be President as any one of them."[155]

Carter, interestingly, openly admitted how difficult it was to play the role of self-assured candidate early in the campaign. In an interview with Robert Turner of the *Boston Globe* in 1974, Carter revealed that "the main difficulty I had to overcome was embarrassment, telling folks I was running for—you know, for President.''[156] But during the course of the long campaign, Carter did become the self-assured candidate. As James Wooten observed:

> ...And it soon became clear that, although his repeated self-assurances of victory were psychological crutches for him, they were also more. He believed them, by God, believed them when no one could or would or should, believed them fervently and passionately and probably more deeply than anyone who had ever had the temerity to tell himself that he really ought to be President of the United States.[157]

By June of 1976, not only was Carter "good" at playing the Presidential candidate role but was conscious of the fact. When asked in an interview if he ever plays a role, Carter responded, "I'm sure I do.''[158]

Once elected, Carter, as with all Presidents, responded with a sense of awe and humility. The office, he stated "calls more for humility than pride, more for reflection than for celebration.''[159] But "becoming" President is a tough task and certainly does not result from taking the oath of office. For Carter, national and international problems compounded almost weekly. Inflation, unemployment, and intense special interest groups were immune to anything his administration attempted to do. Salt II, Cuba, the Middle East, Afghanistan, and Iran all provided "crises" of leadership and tough decisions. By November, 1979, Hugh Sidey had noticed a difference in Carter. He had "become" President even though, some argued, much too late. Sidey noted:

> President Carter looks different. Older, gaunter, grayer, tireder. All that is true. But it is something else.... They have asked themselves exactly what it is—the intensity in the eyes, or the mouth line, or the fractional shift in his jaw set?....But from both the White House and beyond there is testimony that he is more of a President.... "He is challenged from within and from without," says one of his counselors, "that has changed him.''...But that is less important if through some alchemy of these past weeks Jimmy Carter has joined the Presidential club, likes it in there, and wants to stay there badly enough to change himself. We all benefit.[160]

Gerald Ford, in his memoirs *A Time to Heal,* reveals very much the same process. During the spring and summer of 1973, Ford's aids would comment on his eventually becoming President but Ford "brushed it off, partly because I didn't want to believe it.''[161] But when Alexander Haig confronted Ford with the "new evidence" revealed in the tapes of June 23, 1972, Ford had to start assessing his capabilities for the office. He was forced to become an "object" for comparison and evaluation.

> For several minutes after Haig left, the implications of our conversa-
> tion weighed heavily on me. Nixon was going to leave one way or the
> other. The only questions were when and how. And I was going to
> become President — a job to which I'd never aspired.... I'm not the
> kind of person who is torn by self-doubt, and I had no doubts about
> my ability to function well in the office.[162]

After evaluation and often adaptation, acceptance follows. One reacts
according to self-perception of the office as well as public expectations of
the office. When Nixon told Ford of his decision to resign, Ford reportedly
responded, "Mr. President you know that I'm saddened by this circum-
stance. I would have wanted it to be otherwise, but I am ready to do the job
and think I'm fully qualified to do it."[163] Upon leaving the White House
after the above exchange, Ford reports, "Nor did I glance at the Secret
Service Agents accompanying me because I was afraid my feelings might
show. I stared ahead at the car, and I wanted the agents to open the door as
soon as possible so I could climb inside. I needed to be alone."[164] Likewise,
Ford too felt a sense of awe and the imposing nature of the office upon
inauguration.

> As I waited for the proceedings to begin, I felt a sense of awe. It was
> different from the feeling I'd had when I took my oath as a member of
> Congress in 1949 or even as Vice President in 1973. At this historic
> moment, I was aware of kinship with my predecessors. It was almost as
> if all of America's past Presidents were praying for me to succeed.[165]

Despite Nixon's subsequent "overidentification" with the office, he too
initially had doubts.

> As I anticipated becoming President, I found that I was awed by the
> prospect but not fearful of it. I felt prepared. I had the advantage of
> experience and of the detachment that comes from being out of office.
> The "wilderness years" had been years of education and growth.[166]

But as the rest, he also became convinced of his ability to meet the challenges of the office.

> I had no illusions about either the difficulty of the challenge or about
> my ability to meet it. I felt I knew what would *not* work. On the other
> hand, I was less sure what *would* work. I did not have all the answers.
> But I did have definite ideas about the changes I felt were needed.[167]

For Kennedy, according to Schlesinger, "becoming" President
encompassed more than a year.

> What one noticed most was the transformation of Kennedy himself
> from the vigorous but still uncertain figure of early September to a
> supremely assured and powerful leader.... He had changed somewhat
> physically in this year and a half. The face was more lined and furrowed;

the features were heavier, less handsome but more powerful. The first eighteen months is always the period of Presidential definition, and for Kennedy the succession of crises had tied an already disciplined personality ever more irrevocably to the responsibilities for which he held himself accountable to the future.[168]

But some Presidents did not have the luxury of months of campaigning to evaluate and adapt themselves for the job of President. Tragedy demanded immediate assessment and instant acceptance. Truman, after suddenly being told of Roosevelt's death, wrote "During those first few hours, painful as they were because of our tragic loss, my mind kept turning to the task I had inherited and to the grave responsibilities that confronted our nation at that critical moment in history."[169] Johnson articulately states the immediate role requirements of suddenly becoming President.

> Most of all I realized that, ready or not, new and immeasurable duties had been thrust upon me. There were tasks to perform that only I had the authority to perform. A nation stunned, shaken to its very heart, had to be reassured that the government was not in a state of paralysis. I had to convince everyone everywhere that the country would go forward, that the business of the United States would proceed. I knew that not only the nation but the whole world would be anxiously following every move I made — watching, judging, weighing, balancing.[170]

It is interesting to note how former Presidents recall the first time being addressed as "Mr. President." Nearly all of them emphasize how special the moment was while being cognizant of the implications. John Mitchell was with Nixon when the networks began declaring Nixon as the winner of the Presidential race. Nixon recalls:

> I put a hand on John Mitchell's shoulder and said, "Well, John, we had better get down to Florida and get this thing planned out." Before Mitchell could respond, tears welled up in his eyes. He said very quietly, "Mr. President, I think I'd better go up to be with Martha." This was a doubly moving moment for us both. It was the first time that anyone addressed me by the title I had just won.[171]

At the hospital in Dallas, Assistant Press Secretary Malcolm Kilduff addressed Johnson as "Mr. President." Johnson writes, "This was the first time anyone had called me that and I must have looked startled; I certainly felt strange."[172]

Presidential memoirs, similarly, express the forbidding, isolating nature of the office. Even among the closest of friends, the Presidency imposes and invades upon any relationship. When Johnson's friends stood up upon his arrival on Air Force One, the event signaled a profound change to Johnson.

> It was at that moment that I realized nothing would ever be the same again. A wall-high, forbidden, historic — separated us now, a wall that

> derives from the office of the Presidency of the United States.... To old friends who had never called me anything but Lyndon, I would now be "Mr. President." It was a frightening disturbing prospect. I instinctively reached for Lady Bird's hand for reassurance.[173]

Eisenhower touchingly recalls,

> ...my first full day at the Presidential desk — my old friend General Omar Bradley, then chairman of the Joint Chiefs of Staff, phoned me. For years we had been "Ike" and "Brad" to each other. But now, in the course of our conversation, he addressed me as "Mr. President." Somehow this little incident rocked me back on my heels. Naturally, I know all about Presidential protocol, but I suppose I had never quite realized the isolation that the job forces upon a man.[174]

For Truman, the enormous responsibilities of the office contributed to the isolation of the job. "No one who has not had the responsibilities can really understand what it is like to be President, not even his closest aides or members of his immediate family. There is no end to the chain of responsibility that binds him, and he is never allowed to forget that he is President."[175]

In this discussion, several elements of the interaction of the office with the office holder have been emphasized. First, clearly the Presidency, as an office, has a profound influence upon any occupant. Each President must become an "object" subject to self evaluation, assessment, and comparison. In "becoming" President, an individual must respond to self, as well as public expectations and perceptions of the office. This often requires adoption and adaptation of certain perceived qualities and characteristics occurring over a period of time. Finally, from an interactionist perspective, one can better appreciate the "process" nature of the interaction of an individual with the office. Consequently, the impact and influence of the office upon the "self" of an individual is revealed.

Conclusion

This chapter has focused on two dimensions of interaction. The interaction of the office of President with the public and the interaction of the office with the office holder. In discussing the interaction of the office with the public, it was helpful to distinguish among Presidential functions, roles, and models. Presidential functions are specific tasks or duties required of the office. Presidential functions transcend individual Presidents and are generic to the office. A President may select many roles to carry out or perform the tasks of the office. Roles, then, are the medium of performing specific duties. A successful role set or pattern may produce a model of behavior. These distinctions are useful in recognizing that there are many more roles from which to choose than generic functions of the office. If a role set is liked, it may well become a pattern for future Presidential behavior. As the Presidency becomes more complex so does the number of models and the number of roles. Correspondingly, as the number of roles increases so do expectations of Presidential performance. In addition, societal expectations can, in turn, create political roles. Thus, the office of President has grown because of the interaction of the office with the public and the public with the office. As public expectations increase, so does the job. Concurrently, the job is forced to expand to meet public expectations.

There are a whole host of expectations. They tend, however, to focus on the office and the individuals who occupy the office. Generally, the office commands a great deal of support and respect. It is the peak of American political life. The occupant is expected to take care of the needs of the citizens, be a competent manager of government, and provide a sense of legitimacy. The "laundry list" of personal qualities a President should possess is vast and largely a product of "wishful thinking." Candidates are forced, therefore, to create the impressions of meeting the expected and desired qualities. The public's inflated expectations and demands of the Presidency invite paradoxical, two-faced behavior. False expectations invite Presidents to overpromise and overextend themselves, ultimately resulting in public disappointment and disillusionment. Yet, role expectations of Presidential behavior and performance are a product of complex lifelong socialization. The office, as perceived, meets rather specific psychological needs of the populace.

Such pervasive influences of the office over people naturally leads to a discussion of power. This chapter suggests that Presidential power has largely been exaggerated. Power really results from getting others to accept one's view and perspective of reality. To do so, one must control, influence, and sustain one's own definition of the situation by "acting" which creates an image that ultimately leads others to voluntarily behave in the desired way.

Finally, this chapter attempted briefly to view the impact of the office upon the office holder. The "political self" must be isolated, interpreted, and defined socially. The "political self" involves continual mediation between one's own impulses and the expectations of others. Each President confronts the "role" and must adapt to the office. One notices, first, a comparison process whereby the individual assesses his capabilities of being President. Next, one finds considerable speculation as to the awe when one is President. Finally, as a result of interacting with the public, historical expectations, and individual views of the office; the person "becomes" President.

The level of interaction investigated in this chapter is most critical and complex. It is this level of interaction that "gives" the institution "life."

Such a perspective better enables one to view how Presidential roles are created, sustained, and permeated over time throughout society. Consequently, the perspective emphasizes the mythic, paradoxical development of the office plus the fact that the Presidency is "greater" than any individual holding the office.

Footnotes

[1] I, of course, recognize the needs and benefits of "disciplines." If, however, one believes in "absolute," "hard," "cold" facts or "reality"; then this entire study will not only be confusing, but equally frustrating. If this is the case, I suggest "exposure" to the notions of general semantics. This will increase appreciation for symbolic interaction and this study.

[2] Although Political Scientists have used the term "role" for many years, they have not been true to the concept as developed in social psychology. Perhaps one of the earliest successful attempts at utilizing the term in its "proper" way is Richard Rose, *People In Politics: Observations Across the Atlantic* (New York: Basic Books, Inc., 1965), p. 96.

[3] Norton Long, "The Political Act As An Act of Will," in Paul Tillett, ed., *The Political Vocation* (New York: Basic Books, Inc., 1965), p. 179.

[4] Long, p. 179.

[5] For good concise discussion of these two dimensions see Fred Greenstein, "What the President Means to Americans: Presidential 'choice' Between Elections" in James D. Barber, ed., *Choosing The President* (Englewood Cliffs: Prentice Hall, Inc., 1974), pp. 121-147.

[6] David Haight and Larry Johnston, *The President: Roles and Powers* (Chicago: Rand McNally, 1965), p. 366.

[7] Clinton, Rossiter, *The American Presidency,* 2nd Ed., (New York: Mentor Book, 1960), pp. 72-75. See also Charles C. Thach, *The Creation of the Presidency* (Baltimore: The Johns Hopkins Press, 1969).

[8] For a good discussion of the Constitution see Thomas J. Norton, *The Constitution of the United States: Its Sources and Its Application* (New York: Committee for Constitutional Government, 1965).

[9] Thomas Cronin, *The State of the Presidency* (Boston: Little, Brown, and Co., 1975), pp. 250-256.

[10] Bruce Buchanan, *The Presidential Experience* (Englewood Cliffs: Prentice-Hall, 1978), pp. 16-17.

[11] George Reedy, *The Twilight of the Presidency* (New York: World Publishing, 1970), p. 29.

[12] Edward S. Corwin, *The President: Office and Powers,* 3rd. Ed. (New York: New York University Press, 1948), pp. 20-23.

[13] Rossiter, pp. 28-37.

[14] Myron Hale, "Presidential Influence, Authority, and Power and Economic Policy" to be published in a *Festschrift* in honor of Francis D. Wormuth. The selection is also contained in the author's forthcoming book on "The President and the Policy Process," p. 10.

[15] James Burns, *Presidential Government: The Crucible of Leadership* (Boston: Houghton Mifflin Co., 1965), pp. 108-109.

[16] *Ibid.*, pp. 111-112.

[17] *Ibid.*, pp. 112-114.

[18] *Ibid.*, p. 29.

[19] Sidney Hyman, "What is the President's True Role?" in David Haight and Larry Johnston, eds., *The President: Roles and Powers* (Chicago: Rand McNally Co., 1965), pp. 32-34.

[20] *Ibid.*, p. 33.

[21] *Ibid.*

[22] Richard Pious, *The American Presidency* (New York: Basic Books, 1979), pp. 12-13.

[23] *Ibid.*, p. 13.

[24] Hale, pp. 2-3.

[25] See Cronin, Pious, and Hale.

[26] Cronin, p. 33.

[27] Don Faules and Dennis Alexander, *Communication and Social Behavior: A Symbolic Interaction Perspective* (Mass: Addison-Wesley Publishing Co., 1978), p. 67.

[28] As stated in Faules and Alexander, p. 67.

[29] Rose, p. 110.

[30] Cronin, p. 34.

[31] *Ibid.*, p. 35.

[32] Emmet J. Hughes, *The Living Presidency* (New York: Penguin Books, 1972), p. 26.

[33] Rose, p. 111.

[34] Murray Edelman, *Politics as Symbolic Action* (Chicago: Markham Publishing Co., 1971), p. 55.

[35] *Ibid.*, p. 55.

[36] Alfred de Grazia, "The Myth of the President" in Aaron Wildavsky ed., *The Presidency* (Boston: Little, Brown, and Co., 1969), p. 50.

[37] *Ibid.*

[38] David Easton, *A Systems Analysis of Political Life* (New York: Wiley, 1965), pp. 273-274.

[39] *Ibid.*, p. 274.

[40] *Ibid.*

[41] Lester Seligman and Michael Baer, "Expectations of Presidential Leadership in Decision-Making" in Aaron Wildavsky, ed. *The Presidency* (Boston: Little, Brown, and Co., 1959), p. 28.

[42] Louis Brownlow, "What We Expect the President to Do" in Aaron Wildavsky, ed., *The Presidency* (Boston: Little, Brown, and Co., 1969), p. 36.

[43] As reported in Fred Greenstein, p. 125.

[44] *Ibid.*, p. 126.

[45] *Ibid.*, p. 127.

[46] Probably the first major critic which received acclaim was Arthur M. Schlesinger, Jr. *The Imperial Presidency* (Boston: Houghton Mifflin Co., 1973).

[47] Jim Bishop, *A Day in the Life of President Johnson* (New York: Random House, 1967), p. 271.

⁴⁸For example, see how closely these basic general expectations are recognized by Louis Brownlow, p. 36; Cronin, p. 4; and James Barber, *The Presidential Character: Predicting Performance in the White House* (Englewood Cliffs: Prentice-Hall, 1972), p. 9.

⁴⁹Rossiter, pp. 172-174.

⁵⁰*Ibid.,* p. 172.

⁵¹Hughes, pp. 107-134.

⁵²As quoted in Hughes, p. 312.

⁵³*Ibid.,* p. 315.

⁵⁴*Ibid.,* p. 364.

⁵⁵*Ibid.,* p. 278.

⁵⁶*Every Four Years: A Study of the Presidency.* Public Broadcasting Service, 1980, p. 5.

⁵⁷*Ibid.,* p. 11.

⁵⁸*Ibid.,* p. 24.

⁵⁹*Ibid., p. 17.*

⁶⁰Louis W. Koenig, *The Chief Executive* (New York: Harcourt, Brace and World, 1964), p. 6.

⁶¹*Ibid.*

⁶²Thomas Cronin, "The Presidency Public Relations Script" in Rexford Tugwell and Thomas E. Cronin, eds., *The Presidency Reappraised* (New York: Praeger Publishers, 1974), p. 168.

⁶³For the most concise list of paradoxes in a single source, see Thomas Cronin, "The Presidency and Its Paradoxes" in Thomas Cronin and Rexford Tugwell, eds., *The Presidency Reappraised, Second Edition* (New York: Praeger Publishers, 1977), pp. 69-85. Consequently, I relied on his list for this section.

⁶⁴*Ibid.,* p. 72.

⁶⁵*Ibid.,* p. 75.

⁶⁶*Every Four Years,* p. 46.

⁶⁷Niccolo Machiavelli, *The Prince,* translated by Mark Musa (New York: St. Martin's press, 1964), p. 145, 149, 185, 155.

⁶⁸For a good discussion of political roletaking see Murray Edelman, *The Symbolic Uses of Politics* (Urbana: University of Illinois Press, 1964).

⁶⁹*Ibid.,* p. 188.

⁷⁰Rose, p. 99.

⁷¹Faules and Alexander, p. 71.

⁷²Rose, p. 114.

⁷³Faules and Alexander, p. 72.

⁷⁴Rose, p. 104.

⁷⁵Barber, *Presidential Character,* p. 450.

⁷⁶Henry Kariel, *The Promise of Politics* (Englewood Cliffs: Prentice-Hall, 1966), p. 1.

⁷⁷For such an orientation to political behavior see Dan Nimmo, *Political Communication and Public Opinion in America* (California: Goodyear Publishing Co., 1978).

⁷⁸Kenneth Burke, *Language as Symbolic Action* (Berkely: University of California Press, 1966), especially pp. 3-24.

[79]The impact of significant symbols in terms of direct behavior will be discussed in the next chapter.

[80]Nimmo, pp. 227-228.

[81]Greenstein, "What the President Means to Americans," pp. 121-147 and Fred Greenstein, "Popular Images of the President" in Aaron Wildavsky, ed., *The Presidency* (Boston: Little, Brown and Co., 1969), pp. 287-295.

[82]David Easton and Robert Hess, "The Child's Political World," *Midwest Journal of Political Science,* No. 3 (August 1962), p. 231.

[83]Greenstein, "What the President Means to Americans," p. 129.

[84]Easton and Hess, pp. 241-242.

[85]Greenstein, "What the President Means to Americans," p. 134.

[86]For a good, concise review of these see Bruce Campbell, *The American Electorate* (New York: Holt, Rinehart, and Winston, 1979).

[87]William Mullen, *Presidential Power and Politics* (New York: St. Martin's Press, 1976), p. 114.

[88]Campbell, p. 78.

[89]Doris Graber, "Personal Qualities in Presidential Images: The Contribution of the Press," *Midwest Journal of Political Science,* 16 (February), 1972, p. 142.

[90]Greenstein, "Popular Images of the President," p. 292.

[91]Pious, p. 6.

[92]Grant McConnell, *The Modern Presidency* (New York: St. Martin's Press, 1976), p. 19.

[93]*Ibid.,* p. 21.

[94]As quoted in Pious, p. 90.

[95]James Wooten, *Dasher: The Roots and Rising of Jimmy Carter* (New York: Warner Books, 1978), p. 35.

[96]As quoted in Pious, p. 91.

[97]Wooten, p. 277.

[98]McConnell, p. 39.

[99]William Mullen, *Presidential Power and Politics* (New York: St. Martin's Press, 1976), pp. 2-3.

[100]Harold Lasswell, *Psychopathology and Politics* (Chicago: University of Chicago Press, 1930).

[101]His findings are usually contained in any book on the Presidency. In addition, Greenstein has written many articles on the subject expressing the six basic psychological uses of the Presidency. For rather concise statements see: Greenstein, "Popular Images of the President" and "What the President Means to Americans."

[102]Rossiter, p. 79.

[103]One of the best studies on the Cuban Missile Crisis which illustrates this notion is Graham T. Allison, *Essence of Decision* (Boston: Little, Brown, and Co., 1971).

[104]For a concise statement of these approaches see Pious, pp. 15-16.

[105]Rossiter, pp. 41-69.

[106]*Ibid.,* p. 43.

[107]Richard Neustadt, *Presidential Power* (New York: John Wiley and Sons, 1960), p. 28, 122.

[108]*Every Four Years,* p. 45.

[109]Neustadt, p. 2.

[110]Hale, pp. 15-24.

[111]*Ibid.,* p. 16.

[112]*Ibid.,* p. 20.

[113]Koenig, p. 5.

[114]*Ibid.,* p. 5.

[115]Hugh Sidey, "Shadow Dancing with the World," *Time,* December 31, 1979, p. 20.

[116]Theodore H. White, *The Making of the President 1960* (New York: Atheneum Publishers, 1961), p. 371.

[117]White, p. 367.

[118]*Every Four Years,* p. 45.

[119]McConnell, p. 82.

[120]Pious, p. 16.

[121]McConnell, p. 6.

[122]*Every Four Years,* p. 49.

[123]Wildavsky, *The Presidency,* p. xi.

[124]As quoted in Rossiter, p. 149.

[125]Peter Hall, "A Symbolic Interactionist Analysis of Politics," *Sociological Inquiry,* 1972, 42 (3-4), p. 61.

[126]*Ibid.*

[127]See Hale, "Presidential Influence, Authority, and Power and Economic Policy."

[128]Nicholas von Hoffman, *Make-Believe Presidents: Illusions of Power from McKinley to Carter* (New York: Pantheon Books, 1978), p. 225.

[129]Gordon Tullock, *The Politics of Bureaucracy* (Washington: Public Affairs Press, 1965), p. 131.

[130]Marvin E. Olsen, *The Process of Social Organization* (New York: Holt, Rinehart, and Winston, 1968), p. 173.

[131]Edelman, *Politics as Symbolic Action,* p. 31.

[132]Perry London, *Behavior Control* (New York: Meridian Books, 1977), p. 36.

[133]*Ibid.,* p. 27.

[134]Chester Cooper, *The Last Crusade: America in Vietnam* (New York: Dodd, Mead, 1970), p. 416.

[135]The idea of the Quadrants and labels were stimulated by John Orman's *Presidential Secrecy and Deception: Beyond the Power to Persuade* (Connecticut: Greenwood Press, 1980) and his discussion of Presidential secrecy and deception. Thus, the openness-secrecy dimension is borrowed from his work as well as some of the quadrant labels.

[136]For a complete account, see Allison.

[137]See Neustadt.

[138]See John Kotter, *Power in Management* (New York: AMACOM, 1979) for a clear distinction among power, power-oriented behavior, and power dynamics. Although an applied book for managers, his distinctions are developed well.

[139]White, p. 367.

[140]Nimmo, pp. 313-314.

[141]*Every Four Years,* p. 69.

[142]Reedy, p. 15.

[143]*Ibid.,* p. 16.

[144]George Reedy, "On the Isolation of Presidents," in Thomas Cronin and Rexford Tugwell, eds., *The Presidency Reappraised: Second Edition* (New York: Praeger Publishers, 1977), p. 194.

[145]See Buchanan.

[146]*Ibid.*, p. 18.

[147]*Ibid.*, p. 138.

[148]Hugh Dalziel Duncan, *Symbols in Society* (New York: Oxford University, 1968), p. 19.

[149]Arthur Schlesinger, *A Thousand Days* (Greenwich: A Fawcett Premier Book, 1965), p. 100.

[150]Schlesinger, p. 101.

[151]*Ibid.*, p. 113.

[152]Doris Kearns, *Lyndon Johnson and the American Dream* (New York: Harper & Row, 1976), p. 180.

[153]James Wooten, p. 296.

[154]Jimmy Carter, *Why Not the Best* (New York: A Bantam Book, 1975), pp. 158-159.

[155]Robert L. Turner, *"I'll Never Lie To You:" Jimmy Carter In His Own Words* (New York: Ballantine Books, 1976), p. 63.

[156]*Ibid.*, p. 3.

[157]*Wooten, p. 21.*

[158]Turner, p. 65.

[159]*Ibid.*, p. 2.

[160]Hugh Sidey, "The Presidency: Change in the Set of the Jaw," *Time*, Nov. 12, 1979, p. 26.

[161]Gerald Ford, *A Time To Heal* (New York: Harper and Row, 1979), p. 5.

[162]*Ibid.*, p. 5.

[163]*Ibid., p. 28.*

[164]*Ibid.*, p. 30.

[165]*Ibid.*, p. 40.

[166]Richard Nixon, *The Memoirs of Richard Nixon* (New York: Grosset and Dunlop, 1978), p. 361.

[167]*Ibid.*

[168]Schlesinger, p. 11 and p. 609.

[169]Harry S. Truman, *Memoirs: Years of Decisions, Vol. I* (New York: Doubleday, 1955), p. 11.

[170]Lyndon B. Johnson, *The Vantage Point* (New York: Holt, Rinehart, and Wilson, 1971), p. 12.

[171]Nixon, pp. 333-334.

[172]Johnson, p. 11.

[173]*Ibid.*, p. 13.

[174]Dwight D. Eisenhower, "Some Thoughts on the Presidency" in Robert Hirschfield, ed., *The Power of the Presidency* (Chicago: Aldine Publishing Co., 2nd Ed., 1973), p. 118.

[175]Truman, p. 1.

Chapter 4

"Mind" and the Interaction
of the Presidency and Society

Introduction

What is government? Is it a set of laws, people, institutions, or specific functions? Where is government? Is it the White House, Capitol, Supreme Court, Pentagon, etc.? These very simple questions illustrate the abstract and pervasive nature of the concept "government." Countless books on "government" identify concrete institutions and specific functions. Yet, "government" is obviously more than any one building, single statute, or individual. Rather, it is an orientation, a view, a process which influences in many subtle ways beliefs, attitudes, values, and consequently behavior. Microscopic analyses abound attempting to isolate specific elements of "government." Macroscopic analyses are needed which focus on the interrelationship between society and "government" as well as "government" and society. From this perspective the concepts of "politics" and "government" encompass more than the end products or "outputs" of any system. Rather the "act" of "politics" and "government" are reciprocal, processual, and pervasive in nature. "Politics," according to Nimmo, "extends to any activity that regulates human conduct sufficiently to ensure that other, nonpolitical activities continue."[1] For him, the purpose of political talk is to "preserve other talk" and thus, "the words of politics consist of far more than those listed in any dictionary."[2] The functions of government — any government — clearly encompass more than regulating behavior through the formulation of laws. More consistent with the perspective of this work is Gabriel Almond's description of the functions of government.[3] He posits that the chief functions of government are: political socialization and recruitment; interest articulation; the aggregation of interests; political communication; rule-making; rule application; and rule adjudication. These functions are of a "quality" nature and demonstrate that even in our current crises the advocating of gas rationing or a massive tax cut is of lesser importance than trust and confidence in the viability of a system of government.

Confronting the above functions of government is the reality that the mechanics of politics is not very salient to the average citizen. The general public has little tolerance for complex problems, detailed solutions, or complicated rationales. "People for whom politics is not important," argues Edelman, "want symbols and not information: dramatic in outline, devoid of detail and of the realistic recognition of uncertainties and of opposing consideration."[4] The importance of this notion, in terms of the Presidency, is the fact that the office is public property. The Presidency truly "represents" more than the office "does." The nation may tire of a specific individual but not the institution. Buchanan notes:

> The traditional Presidency has barrowed deeply into the American psyche and sparked there a visceral and abiding trust in the institution — a trust that apparently cannot be destroyed by an occasional miscreant President. Indeed, the hold of the historical Presidency on the minds of the people may well be the single most important reason for the political stability that distinguishes this government from most others.[5]

For individuals to succeed in the office, Hess argues that all Presidents must develop "dramatic instincts and their appreciation of the mysteries of making news. But all Presidents must find ways to communicate, to persuade the people and to arouse and enlist support."[6] In this nation, the Presidency is a very visible link to and distillation of "government."

When considering the relation of government to society, Rose identifies four criteria which emphasize the importance of government actions for the public.[7] The first criterion is the scope of a government activity. How many individuals of the population are affected by the action? The second criterion is the intensity of the impact of the government's action. In short, how much importance is attached to the action by the public? Third, the frequency of impact of governmental decisions is important. Here, the central question becomes how often or how long are people affected by governmental actions? Finally, probability is the last criterion. How likely is it that a person will be affected by a government policy? If these criteria gage the magnitude of influence of "government" over society, the Presidency clearly tops the list. No other institution singularly spans the nation and encompasses the scope, intensity, frequency, and probability of impact as does the Presidency. As McConnell emphasizes:

> The American Presidency is the most conspicuous office in the world. By reputation also the most powerful office, it sooner or later becomes a focus of every important crisis that afflicts the people of the earth. Its own crises are those of the American republic itself; they often send reverberations across the seas. How it is conducted affects the fates of nations and can tip the scales of life and death for millions.[8]

But such support for any individual, institution, or system of government is not automatic. Societal support is a long, continual, and active process. Perhaps the major task confronting any President and the American government is to generate enough support for Presidential authority and action to meet the needs of all segments of society. "Legitimacy," as defined in David Easton's significant work, is the "conviction on the part of the (citizen) that it is *right* and *proper* for him to accept and obey the authorities and to abide by the requirements of the regime."[9] Legitimacy, according to Easton, is a two-way proposition. It is desirable for citizens because it sustains political order, stability, and consequently minimizes stressful changes and surprises. A sense of legitimacy is advantageous for authorities because it becomes the most significant device for regulating the flow of diffuse support.[10]

Diffuse support demands that a President mobilize the entire nation. To mobilize the nation is to, in the words of McConnell, "give shape, to organize, to create and recreate the nation. The process is inevitably touched with mystery."[11] But this "mystery" for some scholars is nothing more than playing upon the hopes, desires, fears, and myths of the public which are constantly being created as well as reinforced through socialization by the government. Joe McGinniss candidly argues that

> Politics, in a sense, has always been a con game. The American voter, insisting upon his belief in a higher order, clings to his religion, which promises another, better life; and defends passionately the illusion that the men he chooses to lead him are of finer nature than he. It has been traditional that the successful politician honor this illusion. To succeed today, he must embellish it. Particularly if he wants to be President.[12]

This chapter is a discussion of the interaction of society and the institution of the American Presidency. Such interaction clearly influences societal behavior. Behavior, as argued in chapter 2, is based on the process of examination and deliberation of a situation. Lauer and Handel note that an "individual's response in any particular situation is a function of how he or she defines that situation, rather than how the situation is objectively presented to him or her."[13] Thus, by understanding the meaning of a situation or environment for individuals, one may understand the behavior of individuals in a situation or society. Also of importance to this discussion and noted in chapter 2 is the notion of William Thomas that there is always a rivalry between the spontaneous definitions of situations by individuals and definitions provided by society.[14] Symbolic interactionists emphasize the dynamic, changing nature of society. Individuals are constantly interacting, developing, and shaping society.

Specifically, this chapter focuses on how the Presidency affects societal behavior. The office primarily affects behavior by defining and controlling societal situations and social settings. One can view institutional influences upon societal behavior by noticing manipulation of campaign settings, leadership impressions, and the resulting manifestation of social order. In addition, the ways or approaches of controlling settings by the Presidency are investigated. For far too long, American political institutions have been considered the embodiment of democracy rather than the mechanism for the achievement of democracy. Democracy is viewed principally as an end product rather than a "means" or process of operationalizing "liberty" or "equality."

Political Setting

Political setting, as defined by Edelman, is "whatever is background and remains over a period of time, limiting perception and response. It is more than land, buildings, and physical props. It includes any assumptions about basic causation or motivation that are generally accepted."[15] The setting, then, creates the perspective from which mass audiences will analyze a situation, define their response, and establish the emotional context of the acts that enfold. The importance of the link between an "appropriate" setting and correspondingly "appropriate" act should be emphasized. Edelman addresses this point in stating:

> The settings of formal political acts help "prove" the integrity and legitimacy of the acts they frame, creating a semblance of reality from which counter-evidence is excluded. Settings also help leaders find the roles and identifications that are significant to followers.[16]

Settings, therefore, condition political acts.

Implicit in this discussion is the need for "government" or leaders to create appropriate political settings which legitimize a set of values. The assumption is, of course, that control over the behavior of others is primarily achieved by influencing the definition of the situation. In a democracy, the secret is to act in such a way that creates an image of the actor or scene which leads others to act *voluntarily* as desired. Although such attempts of "impression management" are frequent, they certainly are not new. In 1928, W.I. Thomas wrote, "If men define situations as real, they are real in their consequences."[17] Getting others to share one's "reality" is the first step toward getting others to act in a prescribed manner. This is best achieved by creating or defining "reality" for others. In turn, the use of potent symbols, rituals, and myths are useful in creating commonalities in the midst of national diversity. The interrelationship of these factors is succinctly described by Nimmo:

> By inducing people to respond in certain ways, to play specific roles toward government, and to change their thoughts, feelings, and expectations, significant political symbols facilitate the formation of public opinion. As significant symbols of political talk, the words, pictures, and acts of political communicators are tipoffs to people that they can expect fellow citizens to respond to symbols in certain anticipated ways.[18]

But certainly the processes defined and described in chapter three are important in terms of ultimate behavior. Individual "appropriate" behavior becomes societal, mass "appropriate" behavior. Presidential persona needs are created, expectations of performance are sustained and permeated, which consequently affect individual and mass behavior. The "phantom" circle is large indeed. Fisher argues that within the images of the Presidential persona lies a part of each of us. For this reason, moving the nation toward specific action is fairly easy. Images of the Presidents are

> symbolic, they not only depict the President, they also imply an image of us; we respond to the implied image of us; we respond to the implied image of us in relation to our self-concept; and the degree to which the implied image and self-concept correspond determines the degree to which we will believe and follow a President.[19]

The entire process, however, yields more than desired behavior. Soon, the process becomes a commitment and total belief in the institutions and system of government. As the myths, images, and symbols are sustained so too are commitment, loyalty, and behavior. The epitome of such commitment and loyalty is best revealed in the statement of H.R. Haldeman, Nixon's White House Chief of Staff:

> I have been accused of blind loyalty to President Nixon both during and since my White House years. I plead guilty to the loyalty, but not to the blindness. My loyalty was, and is, based on a clear recognition of both great virtues and great faults in the man I served. On balance, there has never been any question in my mind as to validity of that loyalty.[20]

If settings and situations are created, the logical question becomes, "How are settings constructed?" In properly answering this question, one must consider, within a dramatistic perspective, the role of language, symbols, myths, and rituals. Such considerations are necessary in understanding how the impact of the institution transcends individual influence to societal influence. Although political symbols, myths, rituals, and talk are all rather commonplace, their implications upon behavior are significant although subtle. Yet, as argued above, they are but one part of the overall "drama." A statement which integrates the elements discussed in the last chapter plus identifies the "goals" and perspective of this chapter is provided succinctly by Walter Fisher:

> It should be borne in mind that the Presidency is an office and a role, an insitution and a persona. At one and the same time, it is symbolic suasory force, a source of inducement to belief, attitude, value, and action; it is a dramatic place, a stage for conflict between heroes and villains, a ground for myth, ritual and legend; it is obviously a position of power and governance; it is a focal point of national reason and rationality; and it is a barometer of public morality and an instrument of humane and inhumane policies.[21]

Role of Language

Socialization depends upon language to mediate the success of a political system's claim to legitimacy. Language is the means of passing cultural and political values. In doing so, language provides a group or individual a means of identification with a specific culture, values, or political entity. As people assess their general environment, language is created which structures, transforms, or destroys the environment. Words are the molds for concepts and thoughts and become symbols reflecting beliefs and values. The creation of language, or symbol systems, is required before societies can develop as well as political cultures. The importance in this regard is noted by Claus Mueller:

> Language provides the opportunity for engaging in social interaction and serves as the main agent of man's integration into a culture.... Jointly shared symbolic expressions which are articulated through language are the means of socialization and create a social bond between individuals and groups since the roles and social relations available in society are transmitted and internalized through language.[22]

Language, therefore, is a very active and creative process which does not reflect an objective "reality" but creates a "reality" by organizing meaningful perceptions abstracted from a complex, bewildering world."[23] It is for this reason that Duncan argues:

> Language must be thought of as a "mode of action" not as an instrument of reflection, for only when we know the situation in which men communicate, and what they are trying to achieve as they communicate (the context of situation) do we know what their expression means.[24]

From this view, language is the means of expressing responses to the physical and social environment. These responses, however, become a mediating force that in turn shapes one's interpretation of the environment. "Metaphorically, language and the words embedded in it," according to Mueller, "are posed between the individual and his environment and serve as an invisible filter. The individual attains a certain degree of understanding through the classification made possible by concepts that screen and structure perception."[25]

Political consciousness is clearly dependent upon language, for language can determine the way in which people relate to their environment.[26] At the very least, language should be viewed as the medium for the generation and perpetuation of politically significant symbols. Political consciousness, therefore, results from a largely symbolic interpretation of sociopolitical experience. To control, manipulate, or structure the "interpretation" is a primary goal of politics in general. The language of government, in many ways, is the dissemination of illusion and ambiguity.[27] A successful politician or leader will use rather specific linguistic devices that reinforce popular beliefs, attitudes, and values. To complete the circle, "politically manipulated language can function as agents promoting the stability — whatever its attributes — of a political order."[28]

From this general discussion, one may argue that most official, Presidential language is an expression of dominant societal symbols and predefinitions. When evoked, rather specific expected behavior occurs. In addition, the use of highly evocative and ritualistic language may indeed structure a political reality which also influences behavior. The paramount questions become whether or not the ritualistic language has any positive effect on the decision-making process and to what extent citizens are "manipulated" by highly abstract, ambiguous rational symbols. It is certainly not the intent of this study to identify all the specific "national symbols." The detailed analysis of any one would easily constitute a sizeable study. Rather, the major concerns here are how these various symbols are created, sustained, permeated in society and their consequential influence upon behavior. For example, the term "national security" was evoked frequently by the Carter administration. The American people were instructed to consume less oil, not to sell grain to Russia, and to support nuclear power endeavors, all in the interest of "national security." Obviously the term became a rather potent linguistic device. However, perhaps what is more important is the "reality" that was created each time the term was evoked; does it make a difference upon behavior if it is evoked by the President, a Senator, or newsperson; what values do the symbol (or term) have resulting from conditioning and socialization? The major concerns, therefore, become how situations are developed, how terms become signficant symbols and how the Presidency as a part of this "process" becomes an influential symbolic artifact affecting societal behavior. To focus on specific "symbols" or policy proposals are of lesser value to this study from an interactionist perspective.

Before discussing specific aspects of language usage vital to Presidential influence, it is useful to identify Edelman's four distinctive governmental language styles.[29] They include: hortatory, legal, administrative, and bargaining styles. As a group, the language styles deal with Presidential authority, persuasion, and participation. Hortatory language is the style most directed toward the mass public. It contains the most overt appeals for candidate and policy support. Consequently, the most sacred of national symbols and values are evoked. Legal language encompasses laws, constitutions, treaties, statutes, contracts, bills, etc. For the citizen, such language is often confusing and intimidating. Because of the ambiguity of the language style, lawyers and judges have a political as well as social function. Legal language compels argument and interpretation. Administrative language is certainly related to legal language. The style usually encourages suspicion and ridicule by the public. Interestingly, administrative language, in its attempts to be clear and concise, is often as confusing to the public as legal language. Bargaining language style "offers a deal, not an appeal" and is acknowledged as the real catalyst of policy formation. Yet, public reaction or response politically is avoided. Once a bargain is created, the rationalization of the bargain often assumes the hortatory language style.

Note that these language styles are content free. Carter might utilize the linguistic devices in the bargaining style to win Congressional approval of a grain embargo; the legal style to draft appropriate legislation; administrative style for enforcing or providing the mechanics for operationalizing the legislation; and the hortatory style in attempting to gain public support for the measure. Each style may create a different "reality" and consequential behavior. The "realities" of crisis, confidence, patriotism, and action may all be created to achieve the final goal. For the basic assumption, according to Edelman, is that the public "responds to currently conspicuous political symbols: not to 'facts,' and not to moral codes embedded in the character or soul, but to the gestures and speeches that make up the drama of the state."[30]

Man lives in a symbolic environment. For Mead, "significant symbols" arise through the process of social interaction. A significant symbol is one which leads to the same response in another person that it calls forth in the thinker. Thus, significant symbols are those with a shared, common meaning by a group. Consequently, a political vocabulary of significant symbols may evolve which provides common understandings among individuals. "Through the social construction of significant symbols, political talk provides a common universe of discourse that preserves and enhances the opportunities for people to engage in further talk directed at adjusting their interest differences."[31]

For a group, there are three ways an individual may respond or relate to a significant symbol. There is a content or informational dimension, a selective dimension, and an evaluative dimension reflecting the importance of the symbol. Each of these dimensions is defined through interaction and hence becomes a rather potent motivator for action.

There is a large number of significant political symbols in society. They have evolved, according to Nimmo, in five ways.[32] From authority talk arises laws, constitutions, treaties, etc. which often sanction specific courses of action and provide rationalization for specific political orientations. Power talk usually creates symbols dealing with international politics. Detente, cold war, or national self-determination are such significant symbols. Influence talk provides the domestic creation of significant symbols arising from such sources as platforms, slogans, speeches, or editorials. Often, complex issues, when condensed into a single term or phrase, become a powerful political symbol. Such symbols include: busing, gun control, abortion, law and order, or more recently, energy. Finally, significant symbols arise from the types of objects symbolized such as "democracy" or "old glory."

Cobb and Elder provide a hierarchical typology of political symbols which is most useful.[33] They identify four types of stimulus objects as the universe of political symbols. At the top of the hierarchy are symbols of the political community comprising the community's core values. Old glory, democracy, equality, etc. would fall within this category. The next type includes regime symbols or those relating to political norms of the society. These include concepts such as "due process" or "free enterprise." Third in the typology are symbols associated with formal political roles and institutions such as the President, Congress, FBI, etc. The last type, situational symbols, is comprised of three components. These components include: governmental authorities (i.e., Carter, Muskie, etc.) non-governmental authorities (i.e., Ralph Nader, Common Cause, etc.) and political issues (i.e., inflation, gun control, crime, etc.). Those symbols, high in the typology, are the most abstract and general, whereas those in the lower divisions are more specific. Thus, the abstract political symbols are more encompassing, applicable, salient, and less temporally specific.

Simply to identify the origins and various types of significant political symbols is not enough. The next question for consideration logically becomes *how* are the symbols used to structure "reality" and thus to motivate behavior? For Nimmo, governmental groups and individuals use political symbols to "assure people that problems are solved even if current policies actually achieve relatively little" and to "arouse and mobilize support for action."[34] The use of euphemism, puffery, and metaphor are vital in creating a sense of assurance. During the Ford Administration, the word "detente" was avoided because it had become associated with a controversial policy. Carter was consistent in referring to the Iranian students as "terrorists" to label their action. Puffery attempts to exaggerate or to overstate matters of subjective experience. In election years, every issue is of the "gravest importance to the future of our country." Metaphor, as a language device, is useful for explaining the unfamiliar by associating it with something more immediate, clear, or known. A "war on poverty" or a war on "crime" reveals a degree of seriousness, priority, and intensity. Simply labelling a problem a "crisis" often mobilizes support. Appeals to "national good" and "self-sacrifice" induce cooperation and support which may restrain free choice. Myth and ritual, which will be viewed later, are potent language forms in arousing public action.

In addition to the above uses of political symbols to influence behavior, Novak argues that a President has a great deal of symbolic power consisting of five components: identification, interests, action, moral fulfillment, and authority.[35] These components focus on the extent an individual, looking at the President, says "we"; the degree a President suggests knowledge and concern for the public's interests; the degree a President's actions stimulate actions in the general public; the degree that a President conveys a sense of admiration and inspiration; and the extent to which a President appears to know what he is doing as well as the ability to direct the nation. Each of these aspects is conveyed through interaction, molded in language, and is more pervasive than any legal power granted in the constitution.

How do political symbols work? It is their abstract, "semantic hollowness" that makes symbols so powerful. Although political symbols function as objects of common identification, they simultaneously allow for individual idiosyncratic meanings to be attached. Two individuals may disfavor abortion but do so based on religious or constitutional grounds. The same two individuals may disagree about abortion for rape victims but clearly support a general appeal by a President disavowing the practice of abortion. Political symbols are powerful not because of the broad commonalities of shared meaning but because of the intense sentiments created and attached to them resulting in the perception that the symbols are vital to the system.[36] Cobb and Elder even argue that the stability of the American polity is a direct result of an abstract, shallow symbolic consensus. "This type of consensus rests upon symbols that are commonly viewed as important and are the objects of relatively homogeneous affective attachments but which lack any commonality of substantive meaning across individuals and groups."[37]

Two symbolic forms that permeate our political life are ritual and myth. As already noted, both are especially valuable in arousing public action. Ritual is "motor activity that involves its participants symbolically in a common enterprise, calling their attention to their relatedness and joint interests in a compelling way."[38] Ritual is the bridge between individuality and society. It functions as a "leveler" providing instant commonality. By allowing one to become a part of a larger entity, ritual promotes conformity in a rather satisfying way.

Myth, in many ways, functions in the same way as does ritual.[39] But myth bridges the old and new. Myth is composed of images from the past that help us cope with the present. Myth reduces the complexity of the world identifying causes that are simple and remedies that are apparent. "In place of a complicated empirical world, men hold to a relatively few, simple, archetypal myths, of which the conspiratorial enemy and the omnicompetent here-savior are the central ones."[40] Virtually all of our political behavior lies in the realm of myth. Barber notes:

> The pulse of politics is a mythic pulse. Political life shares in the national mythology, grows in the wider culture, draws its strength from the human passion for discovering, in our short span of life on this peripheral planet, the drama of human significance. Ours is a story-making civilization; we are a race of incorrigible narrators. The hunger to transform experience into meaning through story spurs the political imagination. We seem bound and determined to find in the mundane business of picking a chief executive a saga of the spirit.[41]

Thus, the greatest American mythic endeavor is to find "a great man" as leader. As a people, Americans find pleasure and comfort in searching as well as in finding heroes. "Two centuries ago," Boorstin argues, "when a great man appeared, people looked for God's purpose in him; today we look for his press agent."[42] Yet, ironically, hero-worship counters democratic dogma. The heart of hero-worship, however, is not reverence for divine qualities but appreciation for popular virtues. Heroes are admired "not because they reveal God, but because they reveal and elevate ourselves."[43] Historical myths are useful for political authorities. They help reinforce "nationalism" and provide a vehicle for diffuse support.

Political symbols are the direct link between individuals and the social order. As elements of a political culture, political symbols function as a stimulus for behavior. They can provide insight into macro- and micro-level behavior. The use of appropriate symbols results in getting people to accept certain policies that may or may not provide tangible rewards, arouse support for various causes, and obedience to governmental authority. For this perspective, "political symbols are means to material and social ends; they are not ends in themselves."[44]

There is, however, a long process from symbol creation, definition, acceptance, and subsequent behavior. For implicit in the argument thus far is the notion that successful leadership and control is dependent upon the successful manipulation of political symbols. There is a constant competition and struggle for national symbols. At one level, a President attempts to manipulate symbols in order to mobilize support, deactivate opposition, and insulate himself from criticism. On a broader level, national symbols are perpetuated in order to preserve the prevailing culture, beliefs, and values. Thus, the ongoing manipulation of political symbols takes place in the context of an existing set of symbols grounded in the political culture. For the cynic, the key to political power and authority is simply a matter of "pushing the right buttons" or manipulating the right symbols. Yet, such a notion should not be easily dismissed especially in a democracy where logic, rationality, and open discussion are greatly valued. Rather, a concern for the conditioned, pavlovian responses to political symbols should be carefully evaluated. Such an investigation of symbol manipulation must consider aspects of cognition, perception, and image creation.

Cognition, Perception, and Image

In attempting to explain social action, Pranger argues that three variables present themselves: experience (symbols), perception (meaning), and a system linking experience and perception.[45] The "linking system," of course, is politics. Political activities attempt to define "experience" thus resulting in a desired "perception." The reverse is also, obviously, possible. Therefore, the "linking system" (i.e., how "experience" and "perception" are linked) is of vital importance yet often ignored. To explain political behavior as resulting from individual rationality, desires, and attitudes is, according to Edelman, simplistic and misleading:

> Adequate explanation must focus on the complex element that intervenes between the environment and the behavior of human beings: creation and change in common meanings through symbolic apprehension in groups of people of interests, pressures, threats, and possibilities.[46]

Thus, the focus becomes one of cognition control and "reality" development.

Can the manipulation of significant political symbols affect beliefs, attitudes, or values? The apparent answer to this question is "yes." However, some scholars would only provide a qualified "yes" to the above question. For example, few scholars agree that "hard-sell" media campaigns alter the attitudes of large numbers of people. The body of research on political socialization and political cognitions is growing.[47] Yet, much of this research has been short term studies. Cognitions dealing with broad, societal concepts such as "the Presidency" develop over long periods of time. The impact, therefore, of media and official appeals may be greater than the current literature proclaims. In addition, many studies tend to distinguish between attitudes and cognitions.[48] Many studies tend to focus on clearly "persuasive messages" while ignoring the subtle effects of "educational messages" upon attitudes. The assumption often is that cognitions can be isolated and measured separately from attitudes. I find myself in agreement, however, with Brecker, McCombs, and McLeod in asking, "Is there any real difference among attitudes, values, and opinions?...The distinction between cognition and attitude becomes hazy at times."[49] For the purposes of this study, it is perhaps more profitable to recognize that "persuasion and attention are complex processes in which symbols, myths, and reality-testing are all components...."[50] From the public perspective, people interpret messages in such a way that is compatible with long term commitments, with the beliefs created by events (or drama), and with the current (i.e., believable) "reality."

A "structured consensus" is usually believed to be one that is either formed by a group of political elites and transmitted to the public that must accept the decisions or one that is formulated based on the nature of the political-economic system.[51] Consequently, few scholars would argue that in America consensus is so stringently engineered or structured. Even those advocating a "pluralist-elite" orientation acknowledge that special interest groups that may influence policy "come and go." Yet, surely attempts to structure consensus exist in this country—albeit often subtle, pervasive, and long term. More useful, such attempts are defined as "political impression management."[52] Political impression management takes two basic forms. One form is simply to control the flow and amount of information. The belief here is that "knowledge is power." In America, major corporations utilize this approach. The most noticeable recent attempts are those of the oil companies. They attempt to deemphasize quarterly profit reports plus spend huge sums "educating" the public as to the "facts" of world oil production. Certainly the Vietnam War spanning from America's initial involvement to the nation's final withdrawal is a classic case of the government controlling information in attempting to create rather specific "political impressions" (i.e., "stable regime," "protecting democracy," "winning," etc.). The second major form of political impression management is the symbolic mobilization of support. Symbolic mobilization of support "calls attention to front-stage performances where symbols, verbal and non-verbal, are used to strengthen or maintain the position of political actors."[53] This is the most potent form of impression management in America.

Public views on issues are mobilized rather than fixed. Issues themselves are largely created, identified, and permeated throughout society. Neither issues nor specific positions on issues exists in a vacuum. Advocates of a "systems or process" orientation to government are mistaken to conceive of "outputs" as public policy "goals." Rather, governmental "outputs" are results of the *creation* of political followings and mass support. This is usually the case when a politician refers to "tapping a reservoir of public support." Obviously governmental activities greatly influence the mobilization of public attitudes and thus support. Such mobilization of support, however, is much easier when revolved around a potent political symbol. Any President can almost justify any action or policy "output" or mobilize public support for a specific policy by defining the issue in terms of "national security." Not only is the concept of "national security" potent, but also the expectations of Presidential performance dictates that the President will take care of his constituents in any emergency; has the best access to needed sources of information in order to make policy decisions; and will always act in the best interests of the nation. "Government affects behavior," as Edelman so masterfully notes, "chiefly by shaping the cognitions of large numbers of people in ambiguous situations. It helps create their beliefs about what is proper; their perceptions of what is fact; and their expectations of what is to come."[54] The principal task becomes, therefore, not to grant public demands but to change or control the demands and expectations of the public. To accomplish this is to control the cognitions and perceptions of the people. And this is best achieved by the manipulation of broad, abstract, national symbols. "In these terms a symbol can be understood as a way of organizing a repertory of cognitions into meanings."[55] Mead argues that expectations influence perceptions and interpretations of ambiguous "facts" influence attitudes.

It is certain to repeat the obvious to note the significant role the mass media plays in providing immediate access of information to the citizenry of the nation—as well as providing powerful techniques of creating and permeating desired "images" for public consumption. A President can, nearly at any time, command the attention of the media and speak directly to the American people. In addition, a President constantly attempts to create a favorable image in the minds of the public. To do so, he must rely on socialized perceptions and expectations of Presidential behavior.

For the purpose of this discussion, the "agenda-setting" model of media influence upon public cognition is the most informative.[56] The model simply argues that the social system has an impact upon media institutions and they in turn influence public perceptions and cognitions. Specifically, media personnel (i.e., reporters, editors, managers, etc.) make decisions, which are influenced by the social system, that have impact on the cognitions of media audiences. Perhaps the classic example of the mutual and interrelationship of government and media impact upon public perceptions is the "pseudo-event."[57] A pseudo-event is a planned, contrived event designed to catch the attention of the news media and thus be widely reported. The events are to "appear" spontaneous and the cameras function only as an unobtrusive window to a situation. The true purpose of such events, however, is to produce favorable images of a specific person or group. To generate pseudo-events is to control the setting by making news flattering to the party involved.

A very significant form of cognition control is a "symbolic belief system" called an "ideology." The function of ideology is to transform listeners into believers and consequently believers into actors. To accept an ideology implies a commitment toward a specific "social reality." On a larger scale, the commitment toward an ideology links one to a community of believers who largely share the same interpretation of the world. Obviously, such a commonality of viewing "reality" provides a strong rationale for specific societal behavior or action.

The foregoing has focused on rather short term modes of governmental influences upon public cognitions. More important, as well as consistent, with the macro orientation of this study is the concern for long term influences upon cognitions in regards to the Presidency. The best single discussion of this aspect is provided in Kenneth Boulding's *The Image*.[58] An "image," for Boulding, is one's perception or subjective knowledge. An image is the result of all past experience plus the history of an image itself. Consequently, all messages are filtered through various images. Raw data from the "real" world are mediated through a rather strictly learned process of interpretation and acceptance.

The dynamics of political images can only be appreciated by understanding the interaction of two key societal processes.[59] The first process is that of political images being created and distributed among the individuals of a society. This study, as a whole, is an attempt to focus on the "presidential image" in the above "process." The second dynamic of political life is the distribution of specialized skills and knowledge among the people of the society. Political images include not only role expectations but also symbolic or personalized images of institutions themselves.

Nearly every American has a rather clear or concrete image of the Presidential role. The image is perpetuated from generation to generation and is modified overtime by agencies of formal instruction and, more importantly, face to face communication.[60] The long term process and dynamics of the Presidential image developed is described by Boulding as

> ...a role image which originated in the minds of the founding fathers and in the course of the long political and constitutional discussions which preceded the founding of this republic. It is an image which is partly enshrined in the transcript of the constitution. It is an image, however, which has been chaging slowly in the course of history and which is derived in part from the recorded experience of the occupants of the role. The role is the center of a complex network of communications both in and out, part of which each occupant of the role inherits and part of which he creates for himself.[61]

Many "images" and "perceptions" comprise any situation. These "images" and "perceptions," as already argued, do not exist in a vacuum. Rather, they are created and evolve from the interaction among people, government, and political leaders. Culture is not transmitted like a telegraph message. Culture is taught in human endeavors which are largely created, staged, and performed by people in the community who have been trained and who are, in turn, training others in cultural presentation. Society results from the blending together of the vast separate lines of action of the members of a group. Such a process Blumer calls "joint action." The basis for joint action is "the establishment through interpretive interaction of common definitions of the situation. Even though much of joint action is in the form of repetitive, patterned responses to common situations, each instance of it has to be recreated, reconstituted, and reenacted."[62] A Presidential contest is really a contest of competing definitions of situation. The winner is one who successfully articulates the "definition of situation" held by the majority or one who successfully creates a potent "definition of situation" that has been adopted by a majority of the voters. Such a view of society and situation and consequently politics is grounded in a Dramatistic orientation.

A Dramatistic Orientation to Situation, Society, and Politics

Dramatism, created and developed by Kenneth Burke, is grounded in the symbolic nature of man. Burke argues that as a symbol using animal, one must stress symbolism as a motive in any discussion of social behavior. By 1968, Dramatism was "promoted" to equal status with "symbolic interaction" and "social exchange" as being one of three areas of "interaction" discussed in the *International Encyclopedia of the Social Sciences.*[63] In that article, Burke summarizes Dramatism as

> a method analysis and a corresponding critique of terminology designed to show that the most direct route to the study of human relations and human motives is via a methodical inquiry into cycles or clusters of terms and their functions.[64]

At the heart of dramatism is action. For dramatism is a heuristic for the analysis of human action.[65] An "act" is a "terministic center" from which many related influences and considerations derive.[66] Daily "actions" constitute dramas with created and attached significance. For Burke, drama serves as an analytic model of the social world. "Though a drama is a mode of 'symbolic action' so designed that an audience might be induced to 'act symbolically' in sympathy with it, insofar as the drama serves this function it may be studied as a 'perfect mechanism' composed of parts moving in perfect adjustment to one another like clockwork."[67]

Burke makes a pragmatic distinction between the "actions of persons" and the "motions of things." Action is grounded in the symbolic nature of man whereas motion is grounded in the physical laws of nature. In short, "things move, people act." In order to understand the dynamic and inter-relatedness of action, Burke developed the "dramatistic pentad." The pentad, consisting of five elements, provides a way to view action. It forces one to be aware of the various influences in any situation and how key individuals, groups, or institutions attempt to "construct" reality. The five key terms of dramatism are act, scene, agent, agency, and purpose. As Burke explains:

> For there to be an act, there must be an agent. Similarly, there must be a scene in which the agent acts. To act in a scene, the agent must employ some means, or agency. And there cannot be an act, in the full sense of the term, unless there is a purpose.[68]

The pentad serves as a very elegant organizing function. These dynamic interlocking elements limit alternative courses of action. Such an orientation is valuable in assessing political definitions of situations. As Overington notes:

> As a method, dramatism addresses the empirical questions of how persona explain their actions to themselves and others, what the cultural and social structural influences of these explanations might be, and what effect connotational limits among the explanatory (motivational) terms might have on these explanations, and hence, on action itself.[69]

Consequently, for Burke, the Presidency may be treated "as a 'situation' affecting the agent who occupies it. And the donning of vestments brings about a symbolic situation."[70] From a dramatistic perspective one may argue that the President is always on stage. His behavior, as public performance, must be managed in order to mobilize and sustain support. But even as a skilled "actor," the citizenry are not merely spectators. They interact with the President. The public participates in his actions and shares his "definition of situation."

Novak even argues that:

> so far as his national actions go, they live in him. His acts are theirs. He is their persona. He is the people, not in a sense that subsumes them under him but in the sense that he is their agent, their spokesman, their image of themselves. So long as he has their confidence, its actions have legitimacy and power.[71]

Every situation in which the President is a part becomes an elaborate drama. Even a news conference earmarks a dramatic performance, in contrast to information sharing, where reporters are part of the setting and become instruments for influencing impressions, and opinions.[72] All drama is powerful in the sense that it influences cognitions, perceptions, and hence expectations of Presidential performance or behavior. "The transcending tendency of drama," Klapp argues, "has a creative power to make and break statuses, to give and take prestige, to generate enthusiasm, to involve and mobilize masses in new directions, and to create new identities."[73]

Situations, in general, provide the context or boundaries for drama. Situations are not objectively defined but are created and manipulated. Correspondingly, such creation affects cognitions, impressions, and perceptions of those involved. Any situation is obviously dynamic involving many elements of mutual influence (i.e., act, actor, agency, purpose). Because of the importance (whether "real" or "perceived") of the Presidency, every "presidential situation" or public context is important. Situations are not neutral, thus have the potential of impact. Three examples of very controlled settings include campaign setting, leadership behavior, and societal order.

Campaign Setting

Stephen Hess observes that Presidential campaigns are exercises in political arithmetic in which only 270 electoral votes are needed to win.[74] Thus, a candidate will act in ways that will attract enough voters to reach the magic number. Our political process of campaigning, theoretically, allows a candidate to become attuned to public opinion and test the desirability of various policy proposals. Yet, political scientists reject the notion that political campaigns substantially influence the outcome of electoral contests.[75] They argue that the major factor influencing voter decision is party loyalty. In addition, studies reveal that most voters make up their mind about whom to support before campaigns begin.

Although political campaigns are not a major factor in elections, one should not fail to recognize their value. Nimmo recognizes three functions of campaigns independent of actual elections.[76] First, campaigns allow voters to adjust their perceptions of political candidates to long-term prejudices. Second, campaigns provide a form of "symbolic reassurance" which contributes to the overall stability of the regime. Third, campaigns provide means of participation and thus the feeling of having influence in the governmental control of daily lives.

A campaign may be defined as "the activities of an individual or group in a particular context designed to manipulate the behavior of a wider number of people to his advantage."[77] The setting, therefore, is critical in any election. Much of the general excitement and atmosphere of campaigns are contrived and illusionary. Potent political symbols are utilized to evoke positive and sympathetic response from an audience. Patriotic songs, emblems of nationhood, red, white, blue, a flag, and portraits of past heroes are vital artifacts in any political campaign setting.

Individually, candidates must attempt to project desired and favorable qualities that the public perceives as necessary for holding office. Such qualities often have little relevance to specific policy programs or even less relevance to reality. However, image projection is an important consideration for professional campaigners. The most favorable image is certainly one that reflects qualities of "leadership."

Leadership

Nimmo argues that political leadership "actually refers to a particular relationship that exists between a leader and his followers in specific settings."[78] The focus, today, on modern leadership theory is upon the willingness of followers to follow. There is no set list of "traits" that constitute "leadership" although certain traits are helpful in any specific situation. It is more useful, according to Edelman, to look for leadership dynamics "in mass responses, not in static characteristics of individuals."[79]

In terms of the Presidency, one should recognize the importance of what Klapp calls "symbolic leadership."[80] The real appeal of public officials is what they symbolize rather than what they have done.

> Certain persons have enormous effect, not because of achievement or vocation but because they stand for certain things; they play dramatic roles highly satisfying to their audiences; they are used psychologically and stir up followings.[81]

Symbolic leadership is an emergent phenomenon resulting from the interaction of the public and the politician. As political drama begins, according to Klapp, roles are identified, interpreted, and projected upon the politician and no distinction is made between "what a thing 'is' and what the audiences sees that is." The key, therefore, in becoming a symbolic leader is to take advantage of the dramatic elements in any setting. Settings become drama when "things happen to audiences because of parts played by actors; the function of the actor is to transport an audience vicariously out of everyday roles into a new kind of 'reality' that has laws and patterns different from the routines of the ordinary social structure."[82]

The sources of images or preconceptions people have of the qualities of leadership are vast. There are, however, three major influences upon such leadership construction. First, history rather carefully characterizes past national leaders. Washington was a man of integrity ("the cherry tree"), determination ("valley Forge"), and was democratic (refusal to be "king"). Lincoln was a man of patience ("preserve the union"), forgiveness ("with malice toward none"), and a lover of freedom ("Emancipation Proclamation"). Second, television greatly contributes to the creation of leadership ideals. The open forums give the impression of being able to assess candidate qualities. Finally, leadership qualities are portrayed in dramatic programs and literature. Often voters openly compare the qualities of politicians to those of professional entertainers. Bob Hope, the deceased John Wayne, and Charlton Heston could probably all easily poll a majority of voters. In fact, Walter Cronkite's name occurred in political polls rather favorably as well as mentioned as a Vice-Presidential candidate for the 1980 Anderson Independent Presidential bid.

To control the setting is to influence cognition or impressions which ultimately influence behavior. The more successsful the "drama" the more stable the regime. Especially in America the drama is complex, encompassing many elements. Yet, the elements all contribute to social order. The Presidential actor in the drama obviously has a major part.

Social Order

Social control is usually viewed as a result of institutional influences such as laws, the police, or Congress. But social order is not totally dependent upon "agencies of control." No regime can long survive on a threat of force alone.

Perhaps, one may argue the most important means of social order is communication. For within communication lies the "power" to create and to control the images that legitimize authority. In addition, communication truly joins all people.

> Images, visions, and all imaginings of the future are symbolic forms, for when the future becomes the present, and thus becomes "real" new futures are created to guide our search for solutions to problems in the present which emerge as we try to create order in our relationships.

Social order, according to Hugh Duncan is always expressed in some kind of hierarchy.[84] Hierarchy differentiates people into ranks based on many variables (i.e., age, sex, skill, wealth, etc.). "All hierarchies function through a 'perfection' of their principles in final moments of social mystification which are reached by mountings from lower to higher principles of social order."[85] Thus, the task for authorities is to invest local symbols with universal symbols which transcend local, isolated concerns.

The community "lives" resulting from intense and frequent reenactments of key roles believed to be necessary to social order. "We learn to act, not simply by preparing to act, or by thinking 'about' action, but by playing roles in various kinds of dramas."[86] For Duncan, there are seven basic forms of social drama which include: games, play, parties, festivals, ceremonies, drama, and rites. In terms of government, ceremonies, rites, and ritual are the most formalized types of social drama. Success is dependent upon the elements of glory and efficiency.

> Glory is a dignification achieved through style (a way of life) which inferiors use to identify themselves with superiors. Superiors, in turn, use

styles of performance (their "presence") to move the hearts and minds of inferiors to loyalty and reverence.[87]

Social order, therefore, is legitimized through symbols grounded in nature, man, society, language, or God. When followers, through socialization, have been taught "significant symbols" which uphold social order they require their leaders to "play" their roles within the principles established.

Conclusion

"Situation" is the context for politics. Dramas are enacted within situations that provide legitimacy and continuation of regimes ultimately resulting in social order and control. Situations are not neutral. They are created, manipulated, and permeated throughout society. Consequently, the "definition of situations" is a commodity that politicians compete to control and own. Public cognitions and impressions are influenced by the investment and utilization of "significant symbols" that are emotional, intense, and cultural in nature. Society, therefore, is a dynamic, interacting entity consisting of many levels acting simultaneously.

The Presidency is itself a "significant symbol" also comprised of many levels and elements. The institution influences and affects the beliefs, attitudes, and even values of the public already established through socialization. As an institution, legitimacy is guaranteed and thus deference to Presidential authority is largely a matter of impression management. Presidential elections are also largely a contest for symbolic legitimation.

Finally, such an orientation to "situation" and society views politics as a mere game. Such an argument, of course, is philosophical. Pragmatists would argue that politics is a matter of "life and death." This, of course, is true. Yet, simply to state that Russian roulette is a matter of "life and death" is to ignore that however serious the consequences, it is above all a game. For each rotation of the barrel presents new odds of "life and death." The game clearly has rules and the more one "wins" the greater the status. To some, playing the game is a ritual of courage and manhood. To recognize politics as a "game" consisting of elaborate social dramas is not to encourage a flippant attitude toward government. Rather, it should encourage caution and deliberation. Perhaps such an orientation better enables the asking of "real" questions. Is America willing to fight in Iran for "Mobil Oil?" Is providing government aid to Chrysler securing "free enterprise?" Does "national security" demand a large defense budget, indiscriminate wire tapping, or CIA covert activities? Did the National Guard, at Kent State, kill rioters, protestors, or students? "A rose by any other name would **not** smell as sweet."

Footnotes

¹Dan Nimmo, *Political Communication and Public Opinion in America* (California: Goodyear Publishing Co., 1978), p. 66.

²*Ibid.,* p. 66.

³G. Almond and J. Coleman, *The Politics of the Developing Areas* (Princeton: University Press, 1960), see "Introduction."

⁴Murray Edelman, "The Politics of Persuasion" in *Choosing the President,* ed. James David Barber (Englewood Cliffs: Prentice-Hall, 1974), p. 156.

⁵Bruce Buchanan, *The Presidential Experience* (Englewood Cliffs: Prentice Hall, 1978), p. 159.

⁶Stephen Hess, *The Presidential Campaign* (Washington: The Brookings Institution, 1974), p. 10.

⁷Richard Rose, *People In Politics* (New York: Basic Books, 1970), pp. 196-197.

⁸Grant McConnell, *The Modern Presidency* (New York: St. Martin's Press, 1976), p. 1.

⁹David Easton, *A Systems Analysis of Political Life* (New York: John Wiley and Sons, 1965), p. 279.

¹⁰*Ibid.,* p. 249.

¹¹McConnell, p. 19.

¹²Joe McGinniss, *The Selling of the President 1968* (New York: Trident Press, 1969), p. 26.

¹³Robert Lauer and Warren Handel, *Social Psychology: The Theory and Application of Symbolic Interaction* (Boston: Houghton Mifflin, 1977), p. 85.

¹⁴Jerome Manis and Bernard Meltzer, ed., *Symbolic Interaction: A Reader in Social Psychology* (Boston: Allyn and Bacon, 1978), p. 255.

¹⁵Murray Edelman, *The Symbolic Uses of Politics* (Urbana: University of Illinois Press, 1964), pp. 102-103.

¹⁶*Ibid.,* p. 190.

¹⁷Peter Hall, "A Symbolic Interactionist Analysis of Politics," *Sociological Inquiry,* 42 (3-4), p. 51.

¹⁸Nimmo, p. 69.

¹⁹Walter Fisher, "Rhetorical Fiction and The Presidency," *Quarterly Journal of Speech,* 66, 2, April 1980, pp. 124-125.

²⁰H.R. Haldeman, *The Ends of Power* (New York: Time Books, 1978), p. xii.

²¹Fisher, pp. 119-120.

²²Claus Mueller, *The Politics of Communication* (New York: Oxford University Press, 1973), p. 13.

²³Murray Edelman, *Politics as Symbolic Action* (Chicago: Markham Publishing, 1971), p. 66.

²⁴Hugh Dalziel Duncan, *Communication and Social Order* (New York: Oxford University Press, 1962), p. 34.

²⁵Mueller, p. 16.

²⁶The strongest statement of this notion is provided by Benjamin Lee Whorf. For him, "If a man thinks in one language, he thinks one way; in another language, another way." The structure of language "is itself the shaper of ideas, the program and guide for the individual's mental activity, for his analysis of impressions,

for his synthesis of his mental stock in trade." See John Carroll, ed. *Language, Thought and Reality: Selected Writings of Benjamin Whorf* (New York: John Wiley and Sons, 1956).

[27] Edelman, *Politics as Symbolic Action*, p. 83.

[28] Mueller, p. 19.

[29] Edelman, *The Symbolic Uses of Politics*, pp. 133-146.

[30] *Ibid.*, p. 172.

[31] Nimmo, p. 67.

[32] *Ibid.*, pp. 67-68.

[33] Roger Cobb and Charles D. Elder, "Individual Orientations in the Study of Political Symbolism," *Social Science Quarterly*, June 1972, 53, 1, pp. 82-86.

[34] Nimmo, pp. 83-86.

[35] Michael Novak, *Choosing Our King* (New York: MacMillan Publishing Co., 1974), pp. 29-31.

[36] Cobb and Elder, p. 80.

[37] *Ibid.*, p. 87.

[38] Edelman, *The Symbolic Use of Politics*, p. 16.

[39] For a good discussion see Lee McDonald, "Myth, Politics and Political Science," *The Western Political Quarterly*, 22 (1969), 141-150.

[40] Edelman, *Politics as Symbolic Action*, p. 83.

[41] James David Barber, *The Pulse of Politics* (New York: Norton, 1980), p. 20.

[42] Daniel Boorstin, *The Image* (New York: Atheneum, 1962), p. 45.

[43] *Ibid.*, p. 50.

[44] Nimmo, p. 90.

[45] Robert J. Pranger, *Action, Symbolism, and Action* (Nashville: Vanderbilt University Press, 1968), p. 67.

[46] Edelman, *Politics As Symbolic Action*, p. 2.

[47] For more recent examples see R. Sigel, "Political Socialization: Its Role in the Political Process," *Annals of the American Academy of Political and Social Science*, 361, September 1965; R.E. Dawson and K. Prewitt, *Political Socialization* (Boston: Little, Brown 1969); D.O. Sears, "Political Behavior" in *The Handbook of Social Psychology*, Lindzey and E. Aronson, eds., Vol. 5, (Mass.: Addison-Wesley, 1969), pp. 315-388; J. Dennis, *Socialization to Politics: A Reader* (New York: Wiley, 1973); and S. Kraus, "Mass Communication and Political Socialization: A Reassessment of Two Decades of Research," *Quarterly Journal of Speech*, 59 (Dec.), 390-400.

[48] See W.J. McGuire, "The Nature of Attitudes and Attitude Change" in *The Handbook of Social Psychology*, Vol. 3, Lindzey and E. Aronson, eds. (Mass.: Addison-Wesley, 1969).

[49] Lee Becker, Maxwell McCombs, and Jack McLeod, "The Development of Political Cognitions" in *Political Communication: Issues and Strategies for Research*, Steven Chaffee, et al. eds. (Beverly Hills: Sage Publications, 1975), p. 26.

[50] Edelman, "The Politics of Persuasion," p. 156.

[51] See Mueller.

[52] For a good analysis of this orientation see Hall.

[53] *Ibid.*, p. 58.

[54] Edelman, *Politics as Symbolic Action*, p. 7.

[55]*Ibid.,* p. 34.
[56]For a good explanation and discussion of this model, see Becker, et al.
[57]For the classic discussion of "pseudo-event" see Becker, *et al.*
[58]See Kenneth Boulding, *The Image: Knowledge in Life and Society* (Ann Arbor: University of Michigan Press, 1961).
[59]*Ibid.,* pp. 97-114.
[60]*Ibid., p. 104.*
[61]*Ibid.,* pp. 103-104.
[62]Hall, p. 41.
[63]Kenneth Burke, "Dramatism" in *International Encyclopedia of the Social Sciences* (New York, 1968), pp. 445-452.
[64]*Ibid.,* p. 445.
[65]Michael Overington, "Kenneth Burke and The Method of Dramatism," *Theory and Society,* Vol. 4, No. 1, Spring 1977, pp. 129-156.
[66]Kenneth Burke, "Dramatism" in *Communication Concepts and Perspectives,* Lee Thayer, ed. (New Jersey: Hayden Book Co.), p. 332.
[67]*Ibid.,* p. 340.
[68]*Ibid.,* p. 332.
[69]Overington, p. 131.
[70]Kenneth Burke, *Grammar of Motives* (Berkeley: University of California Press, 1969), p. 16.
[71]Novak, p. 164.
[72]See Edelman, *The Symbolic Uses of Politics,* p. 101.
[73]Orin Klapp, *Symbolic Leaders* (Chicago: Aldine Publishing Co., 1964), p. 257.
[74]Hess, pp. 17-18.
[75]See Bernard Berelson, Paul Lazarsfeld, and William McPhee, *Voting* (Chicago: The University of Chicago Press, 1954), pp. 132-137; Angus Campbell, et al, *The American Voter* (New York: John Wiley and Sons, 1960), p. 78; William Flanigan, *Political Behavior of the American Electorate* (Boston: Allyn and Bacon, Inc., 1968), pp. 98-102; Gerald Pomper, *Voter's Choice* (New York: Harper and Row, 1975).
[76]Dan Nimmo, *The Political Persuaders* (Englewood Cliffs: Prentice-Hall, 1970), pp. 5-6.
[77]*Ibid.,* p. 10.
[78]*Ibid.,* p. 8.
[79]Edelman, *Symbolic Uses of Politics,* p. 73.
[80]See Klapp.
[81]*Ibid.,* p. 32.
[82]*Ibid.,* p. 24.
[83]Hugh Duncan, *Symbols in Society* (New York: Oxford University Press, 1968), p. 48.
[84]See Duncan, *Symbols in Society* plus *Communication and Social Order.*
[85]Duncan, *Symbols in Society,* p. 78.
[86]*Ibid.,* p. 61.
[87]*Ibid.,* p. 205.

Chapter 5

The Symbolic Crisis of the American Presidency

Introduction

From the beginning, I asserted that this is both a communication study and a study of the American Presidency. To the casual reader, however, such an assertion may be perplexing. How can this be a communication study when there appears to be no systematic analysis of Presidential speeches, addresses, or public proclamations? In addition, how can this be a "serious" study of the Presidency when there is little attention given to the behavior of specific Presidents? In answering these questions, one must appreciate the interdisciplinary approach of a communication investigation plus the level of analysis undertaken.

Interaction is the basis for political behavior. Whether one defines politics as power, influence, bargaining, negotiation, or persuasion, interaction is required. The focus of this study has been on the various dimensions and levels of interaction involving the Presidency. The Presidency, as an institution, is veiwed as a symbolic abstraction. The focus has not been on what the office "does" but rather on what the institution "is" and "becomes" through interaction. The levels of interaction include: individuals of the general public, the general public or society, and specific office holders as they mold and shape their behavior to meet the public's expectations of Presidential behavior.

"One of the most difficult problems in understanding political reality," observes McConnell, "is in comprehending the relation between the formal

115

and the informal aspects of the system."[1] Symbolic interaction, as a perspective, provides a rather clear framework for investigating the dynamic, symbolic, and even ephemeral nature of the office. Interaction involves acting, perceiving, interpreting, and acting again. Such interaction gives rise to "reality" and in this case reveals how the office of President is "created" in society through interaction. The Presidency must be defined in terms of public perceptions of the office. Presidential behavior is based on public expectations permeated by interaction through perceptions of the institution. But the "circle of influence" is indeed a "two-way street." For every President, as well as Presidential candidate, attempts to influence, modify, and control public perceptions.

The scope of this particular study is broad indeed, almost of a survey nature. For each level of interaction could easily justify an intense, comprehensive study. Yet, the perspective always demands a broad, encompassing approach. When an abstract term, such as the "Presidency," becomes a condensation symbol and takes on compelling connotations; Edelman argues that "analysis inevitably involves abstraction; but here the analyst avoids affect or stereotyping by regarding his abstractions as fictions rather than truths or hypotheses."[2] For example, an interactionist analysis of the governmental support of Chrysler Motor Company would not focus on such factors as unemployment, use of tax revenue for unemployment insurance, affects on the state of depression, etc. Rather, the major concern would be *why* the public is told to support or not to support the funding. Is support of the measure primarily for re-election votes or the Democratic party's commitment to jobs or to "protect the quality of life" for most Americans? But what about the notion of "free enterprise" and the separation of private business and government? In short, how the proposal is presented and the terms utilized are most important. What national values and symbols are evoked in supporting the clearly apparent contradictory policy? Such questions involve historical, political, sociological, and psychological considerations yet each question comes into being resulting from an "interactional episode."

Currently, there is little argument as to the existence and importance of "symbolic behavior."[3] Scholars generally agree that the dynamics of social values, goals, and communication are crucial in shaping society. Thus, the major problem currently is not whether to study the nature of symbolic interaction but *how* to study it. More importantly, how does one construct models of symbolic interaction which can be applied to the observable data of communication? The purpose of this study is to present a somewhat systematic, theoretical evaluation of the Presidency from an interactionist viewpoint while at least attempting to provide an additional perspective or approach to the study of the American Presidency. In doing so, the approach offers alternative ways to view traditional political concepts as

Presidential roles, models, power, and leadership. The success of such an attempt, however, depends upon the value of the yields, results, or the application of the perspective to the office of President. The yields of this study are three-fold. First, this study should provide a greater appreciation for the Presidency as an institution. The office itself has a tremendous influence and impact upon each citizen. The institution has a "life of its own" independent of the occupants of the office. This study even suggests that when referring to the modern Presidency, the "office makes the man" and not the reverse. Second, this study acknowledges the importance and hence an appreciation for the symbolic nature of the office. Third, when contemporaries are challenging the viability of the office, this study provides a framework for assessing the current state of the Presidency and the potential effectiveness of the institution in the future.

The Symbolic Nature of the Presidency

On each inauguration day history is being made and another chapter of American history is carefully recorded during the next four years. Every detail of Presidential behavior is noted and significance is attached. The nation "joyfully" recalls that Millard Fillmore married his school teacher; that James Buchanan never married; that Grover Cleveland was the only President to be married in the White House; that William Taft was the largest President (6 feet 3 inches and 300 pounds); that John Tyler had fifteen children; that John Adams was the first President to live in the White House; that Millard Fillmore had the first bathtub installed in the White House; that Andrew Jackson was the first President to ride a train; that Abraham Lincoln was the first to make a whistle-stop campaign tour; that Woodrow Wilson was the first to use radio to speak to the nation; that Franklin Roosevelt was the first to be on television; that Dwight Eisenhower was the first to travel by jet; and that there have been twenty-four lawyers, four military men, three teachers, three authors, three farmers, a tailor, a haberdasher, and an actor as Presidents.[4] Why are such trivia "important" to American citizens? Because these men are the leaders of the nation. They are chosen to lead and consequently they are a part of us. "America has provided the landscape and has given us the resources and the opportunity for this feat of national self hypnosis." Boorstin concludes that "each of us individually provides the market and the demand for the illusions which flood our experience."[5] But such "illusions" make it difficult to distinguish between what is truly "significant" and what is merely a matter of curiosity. The overlay of myth and magic on the Presidency makes assessment of the institution most difficult. "The fatal need for personification of society, animation of ideals, and worship of heroes introduces continuous disorder into the matter-of-fact problems of running a country."[6]

Of all the political myths of the nation, Theodore White argues that the supreme myth is the ability of the citizens to choose the "best" man to lead the nation.[7] From this belief followed the notion that the office would ennoble any who holds the office. "The office would burn the dross from his character; his duties would, by their very weight, make him a superior man, fit to sustain the burden of the law, wise and enduring enough to resist the clash of all selfish interests."[8] Thus, the Presidency is a combination of symbol and reality. However, the symbolic dimensions of the office are increasingly becoming more important as the role of mass media has become both "maker and breaker" of Presidents. As Edelman notes, "the symbolic component is more crucial to the degree that people lack meaningful social commitments that provide a benchmark for evaluation."[9] In fact, the manipulation of salient symbols clouds issues and blurs situations resulting in emotionally charged but nebulously defined symbols.[10]

The Presidency as a symbol or image has six characteristics.[11] The "Presidency" is synthetic, believable, passive, vivid, simplified, and ambiguous. As synthetic, the impression of the office is carefully planned, manipulated, and created to serve a specific purpose. Details of leadership become massive strategies. The institution is believable in that it has prescribed meaning, significance, and expectations attached to the symbol. The office is "real" and manifests criteria for each occupant. Yet, the office is passive in the sense that the symbol is an "ideal," a mixture of hope, myth, and fantasy. In being believable, the office as a symbol is vivid and concrete. As the ideal, whatever its composition, becomes publically shared; the office is "real" in its significance and consequences. As is the case with every symbol, however, it is more simple than the object it represents. The intricacies and complexities of the job are reduced to a few broad, general characteristics that are more readily identifiable. Symbols, as simplified, are also ambiguous floating between imagination and reality awaiting people to fill in the gaps and thus to attach personal significance to the symbol. Thus, the Presidency, as a symbol, aims at suggestion, comprehensiveness, the texture of experience, and passional intelligence.[12]

Perhaps the forefathers were aware of the fact that the most practical method of unifying people was to give them a symbol which all could identify. When the symbol is manifested in a person, the efficacy and effectiveness is greatly enhanced. Clearly the President of the United States is the focal point of the political system. As argued in Chapter 4, every action by the President is symbolic because not only is he merely an executive but also a carrier of meaning. What the individual symbolizes to each person or group depends upon the system of interpretation of the person or group.

"Political symbols bring out in concentrated form those particular meanings and emotions which the members of a group created and reinforce in each other."[13] Consequently, "from the beginning to the end of his term in office, his every action is a means by which citizens interpret life in the United States."[14]

Just what are the symbols through which the President communicates to the people? The answer is simply "everything." To provide a laundry list of specific artifacts, phrases, or actions is not important. There is no way to gage the intensity and saliency of every action. For some, whether the President wears a suit or not is important. Even the flag carries many levels of response in the nation. What is more important to understand is what makes various actions of the President symbolic is the cluster of memories and associations inherent in the actions while recognizing that responses differ for different audiences.[15] It is more beneficial, therefore, to speak of the Presidency as a highly symbolic office rather than identifying specific actions or isolated symbolic endeavors of a President.

Such a position, however, should not be viewed as attempting to avoid specifically describing the symbolic nature of the Presidency. The epitomy of identifying the symbolic nature of the Presidency is Taft's often quoted description of the President as "the personal embodiment and representative of (the people's) dignity and majesty."[16] Clinton Rossiter reflects Taft's statement in proclaiming that the President "is the one-man distillation of the American people just as surely as the Queen is of the British people."[17] The office is the symbol for justice, freedom, equality, continuity, and grandeur. The Presidency, more specifically, mirrors "all that is best" about America as perceived by each citizen. In accordance, Cronin notes: "The Presidency is nearly always a mirror of the fundamental forces in society: the values, the myths, the quest for social control and stability, and the vast, inert, conservative forces that maintain the existing balance of interests."[18]

It is a serious mistake, however, to view such a characterization of the Presidency as passive. The very potency of the Presidency as a symbol gives the office purpose and pragmatic nature. Americans expect Presidents to prod, unite, as well as to provide direction and a sense of purpose. As such, the Presidency fulfills the parental functions of supreme leader, guide, and teacher. It is important to note, however, that symbolic power is the precondition of pragmatic power. Much legislation and many programs have failed because they were not symbolically acceptable. The key to success, of course, is Presidential leadership. Not surprisingly, the most frequent complaint of the Presidency since the Vietnam War is the "lack of leadership." But leadership, from an interactionist perspective, is more than effective management and the ability to isolate and derive solutions to problems.

Recognizing the symbolic importance and dimensions of leadership is not to support the old notion that one is "born" a leader or that leadership is simply a matter of "charisma." Rather, "true leadership" is granted by people comprised of their own unique perceptions, needs, and expectations. Klapp distinguishes three levels of leadership ranging from practical doers within social structures to those whose influence is entirely symbolic.[19]

The first level of leadership consists of those who do things without achieving popular images. This level includes such leaders as football coaches, ministers, or corporation presidents. The second level of leadership Klapp calls "dramatic actor." At this level the leader escapes from the limitations within social structures. Impact on an audience is more important than outcomes or results. The final level of leadership Klapp identifies is the "durable symbol" where the leader is institutionalized. "Finding such a niche means that an image has been consolidated and that a symbolic leader has hit upon a permanent function."[20] Any systematic study of leadership reveals how society finds and serves its needs by choosing leaders who best symbolize something that others desire. "The leaders, in the sense that they initiate feelings, orient multitudes, and are used psychologically so that audiences or followings can move to a state of mind, if not a course of action, that would not be possible without the leader's help."[21]

It is in Presidential elections, however, that symbolism is increasingly becoming the most powerful and planned component. A campaign attempts to legitimize the candidate's visions and to demonstrate leadership capabilities. During an election, the nation is not a classroom but a theater; not an event but a saga competing for the symbolic centers of America. Novak describes a Presidential campaign as:

> a contest for the souls, imaginations, and aspirations of Americans as much as for the nation's levers of power. It is also a contest between national self-images. Not infrequently citizens will vote against their self-interests, coldly and economically defined, for the sake of symbols more important to them.[22]

The symbolic significance of campaigns are interwoven with their pragmatic quest for power.[23] One can recall when a single word or phrase may destroy a candidate's chances (Romney's "brainwashed") or give a candidate serious trouble (Carter's "ethnic purity"). An alarming show of personality may damage a campaign as Muskie's tears in New Hampshire, Nixon's rage in 1962, or George Bush's confrontation in the second candidate forum in 1980. Symbolic violations may inhibit electoral success as Stevenson's marital status and Teddy Kennedy's episode at Chappaquiddick. The rich do not always win (i.e., Lindsay, or Connally) and the underdog may just triumph as McCarthy in 1968, McGovern in 1972, and Carter in 1976. Simply stated, the intangibles are many and the realm of the symbolic is important. In electing a President, "we elect the chief symbol-maker of the land, and empower him in the kingdom of our imaginations as well as in the executive office where he supervises armies, budgets, and appointments."[24]

Perhaps the most often used analog in describing the role of the Presidency in America is the link to royalty. As Barber argues, "we elect a politician and insist that he also be a King."[25] But "kingly" treatment of Presidents is one source of trouble resulting in isolation of Presidents from reality.[26] Yet, the continual respect, awe, and deference given Presidents depite recent failures and disappointments are considerable. For Americans, the President both rules and reigns. To think of the Presidency as royalty brings unity and simplicity to the image of government. The role of television contributes greatly to the coronation. "Its cameras need a single actor, seek the symbolic event as the desert hart seeks water."[27]

For Novak, Americans not only elect a King, but also a high priest and prophet.[28] Together, the terms speak to the symbolic importance and influence of the office. For the President is king in the sense of being the symbolic and decisive focal point of national power and destiny. The President is prophet in the sense of being the chief interpreter of national self-understanding and defining future endeavors. He is priest in the sense of incarnating the nation's values, aspirations, and expressing these through his behavior.

Thus, to define the Presidency as principally a symbolic institution is not to lessen the significance and importance of the office. Rather, it emphasizes the subtle impact of the institution upon every citizen. To describe the President as Priest, Prophet, and King is to acknowledge the respect, expectations, hopes, and values of the American people. And the interactionist perspective best reveals the public's response to the institution and their effect upon its nature.

Assessing the Current State of the Presidency

Increasingly, the Presidency has come under attack from politicians, historians, and scholars. Since about 1965, the disenchantment of Presidential enthusiasts has transformed into revisionist attitudes toward the office. The "problem" of the Presidency depends upon who is diagnosing it. Yet, nearly all Presidential observers believe the problems are of crisis proportions. But what, specifically, is the "crisis" of the American Presidency? Many scholars argue that the "crisis" had its origins in the United States' intervention in a civil war in Indochina. Our "modest" intervention grew, in a span of a few years, from a minor distraction in American foreign policy into an engulfing national obsession.[29] Meanwhile, domestically the nation was bombarded by the "crises" of inflation, race, pollution, crime, drugs, energy, and world food shortages. The "crisis" reached its peak with the resignation of a President of the United States. Watergate and Nixon's subsequent forced resignation sparked reflection, by many Americans, on the office of President. Many Americans realized for the first time that "the checks were not checking" and the "balances were not balancing." More specifically,

> The concentration of information, government by secrecy, and war-making without consultation, and the extensive use of executive privilege, executive agreements, impoundment, reprogramming, and wire-tapping angered Congress and upset a substantial portion of the public. Lies, enemy lists, and egregious violation of the rights of privacy and of the judicial process outraged Americans.[30]

Without precedent, in the Watergate crisis, the President and his aides stood accused of violation of constitutional liberties, commitment of criminal acts, and various other behaviors incompatible with recognized democratic processes.

Is the "crisis" of the American Presidency, therefore, simply a "crisis" of the Nixon Presidency? As the current cliche goes, "it didn't start with Watergate."[31] The Presidents of the postwar era have certainly not enjoyed political good fortune despite the "power" and "mysticism" of the office. Of the seven Presidents of this era, from Harry Truman to Jimmy Carter, two declined to run again because of unpopular wars, one was assassinated, one faced the possibility of impeachment, two failed to be elected as incumbents and President Carter faced stiff opposition from within his own party for renomination. As candidate Carter proclaimed in 1976, "the tragedies of Cambodia and Vietnam—the shock, embarrassment and shame of Watergate—the doubt and confusion surrounding the economic woes of our nation have created unprecedented doubt and soul searching among our people."[32] The "imperial Presidency" has become the catch-word for the process of Presidential aggrandizement and institutinalization which began under Franklin D. Roosevelt. Today, many observers believe the office is unmanageable and frightening in consequences. In short, this is a time of fundamental reappraisal of beliefs about the Presidency and its role in American democracy. Indeed, as prophesied by George Reedy in 1970, "... we may be witnessing the first lengthening of the shadows that will become the twilight of the Presidency."[33]

The various proposals of reform are equally as diverse as the definitions of the "crisis." The prescriptions, however, are grounded in the traditional aproaches to the study of the modern Presidency identified in Chapter One. But for the interactionist, the approaches fail to recognize the true essence of the office which lie within the realm of the symbolic and personal aspects of the institution. Such failure is easily seen when considering the solution orientations advocated by the various historical approaches to the Presidency. The following, of course, is not a detailed analysis but a simplified outline of the various approaches to the "crisis" of the Presidency.

Advocates of the constitutional-legalistic approach argue that a constitutional amendment is needed to limit Presidential "power" and abuses. The call is for structural changes which would alter the relationship of the Presidency to the other branches. The most far reaching structural change would be the implementation of a Parliamentary system of government. Nevertheless, this approach asserts that Presidential authority must be explicit and not simply implied.[34]

The "crisis," for institutionalists, lies in the structure of the office. The office isolates the occupant and encourages "imperial" behavior. As structured, the Presidency is not significantly accountable to the public, the political parties, or Congress.[35] What is required are procedural changes which could be written into laws. For example, the Wars Powers Act of 1973 attempts to curtail the capacity of the President to involve the nation in war without letting Congress in on the decision. Of course, the success of even this law is questionable (i.e., Ford's response to the *Mayaquez* incident and Carter's rescue mission in Iran). While most reforms are basically either structural or procedural in nature, other approaches offer different orientations or identifications of problem areas of the Presidency.

Pluralists argue that Presidents are hostage to special interest groups who often advocate policy decisions contrary to national interests. The task at hand is to decrease the access and influence of interest groups and to "break" the "iron triangle" of Congress, lobbyists, and bureaucracy.[36] For such an approach to be successful, more public groups of shared interests must become more vocal and potent. In the past, blacks and "conservatives" have been the most successful in organizing their influence. More recently, Spanish Americans are becoming more potent politically. At one time, it was hoped that the mass media would increase the development and input of various interest groups. This, however, has not materialized.

From a somewhat related perspective, elitists believe that the President is more nearly a simple "caretaker" of national interests. Although a member of the "power elite," the President's influence, authority, and power are severely constrained and restricted. Reflecting a "class orientation," economic elites are the sources of "real" power. In short, social power equals economic power which ultimately equals political power.[37]

Psychological studies, consisting of psycho-biographies and psycho-histories of Presidents, are currently very popular. Various schemes based on the ideas of psychological theorists have resulted in typologies or models for the evaluation of Presidential performance and hence the establishment of preferred personality types. The rationale of such an approach lies in the belief that an understanding of a President's personality and character permits accurate prediction of his ability to assess reality as well as to handle stress. As a nation, therefore, the job is simply to pick the "right man" thus avoiding a "crisis" of leadership.[38]

Scholars in the areas of decision making and systems analysis focus on the deficiency of Presidential decisions. Major decisions are all too often made in a vacuum lacking information and proper perspective. For them, the "cirsis" of the Presidency is really the "crisis" of decision making. A "healthy" environment is needed to ensure good decisions. Surprisingly, scholars have found that in times of crisis Presidents often make decisions based on incomplete or even false information. Does one dare share "bad" news with the President jeopardizing one's own status, credibility or even job? How accurate is the information and how honest are the experts are the critical factors in making a decision. In addition, analysts have recently advocated the need for looking critically at how legislation is implemented. The process of policy impact and implementation may hinder or help in obtaining desired outcomes. By analyzing the policy process, the effect of Presidential directives and initiatives may improve.[39]

The Presidency is more than a managerial office. To speak of reform or change without recognizing the public's perceptions, attitudes, and beliefs about the nature of the office is clearly doomed to failure. Since the founding of the nation, Americans have nearly always favored solving problems by reforming structures. The above approaches all reflect rather mechanistic solutions to the "crisis" of the American Presidency. Increasingly, however, it is becoming clear that structures are only a small part of the Presidency. Structures, in fact, are operated by individuals whose perceptions, beliefs, and attitudes play a significant role in the ultimate uses of the structures. In addition, they exist in a cultural context consisting of specific norms and expectations. Hence, the "crisis" of the modern Presidency goes beyond the constitutional-legalistic questions; the institutional organizational charts; the pressures of economic elites or interest groups; the specialized "inputs" and "outputs" of policy; and the "real" personality of individual Presidents. Rather, the "crisis" lies within the realm of the symbolic. Specifically, the nature of the "crisis" is the gap between the symbolic, mythic, historical Presidential persona and the harsh "realities" and "demands" of today's world. The nation's "mythic," "symbolic" expectations of the office are no longer apropos to meet the challenges of the twenty-first century. Even some of the classic works on the Presidency that highly praised the institution subtly forewarned of impending danger. Clinton Rossiter's 1956 classic "white knight" orientation to the Presidency proclaims at the beginning of the section on the future of the office that "we need no special gift of prophecy to predict a long and exciting future for the American Presidency."[40] Yet, later he acknowledges that "perhaps the softest spot of all in the general health of the Presidency lies in the gap between the responsibility and authority, between promise and performance, in the areas of public administration.''[41] Reedy argues that "as an institution, its only hope for survival is to leave the museum where it operates and plunge into the world of reality; to walk the streets that real men and women walk; to breathe the air that real men and women breathe.''[42] The modern Presidents have proclaimed wars on inflation, poverty, crime, urban decay, pollution, hunger, cancer, and fuel shortages. Yet, the battles are continually lost and the wars are soon abandoned or forgotten. As a result, Americans are becoming accustomed to Presidential promises that go unfulfilled. "The annual unveilings of a President's legislative priorities and programs now have much in common with the Madison Avenue Broadsides that advertise each year's 'spectacular' new line of automobiles. Perceptive citizens are increasingly sensitive to the performance of both.''[43]

The rise of the creation of images blurs the outlines of reality. Today nearly all aspects of our life are subject to the manipulation of images. Consequently, this has resulted in the blurring of knowledge, desires, and expectations. National politics have become, therefore, a game of illusion mistaken for reality; competition for images rather than ideals. A successful President must become even more concerned with images rather than issues. For today issues are used only in terms of projecting the correct image and as a reflection of "genuine concern." Cronin observes:

> delegated responsiblities and inflated expectations so burden the modern Presidency that for it to function as well as it does is a marvel. The gap between expectations and what can actually be achieved inevitably mars Presidential credibility and makes the modern Presidency vulnerable.[44]

All Presidents since Roosevelt have discovered and openly acknowledge that the gap between what they want to do when elected and what they can do once in office is enormous. This is not to argue simplistically that all Presidents or Presidential candidates are liars. Rather, it emphasizes the distinction between winning an election and governing the nation. The former is a process of highly planned, abstract appeals historically successful yet disconnected from the daily pragmatics of governing.

The distinction between "winning" and "governing" has long been acknowledged. George Reedy in 1970, however, powerfully and succinctly argued the case before the American people. His assessment then consisted of a...

> highly pessimistic view that Camelot will not longer suffice—however effective it may have been in the past. As a rallying point for men who would beat off dragons and ogres, it was superb. As a device to lead us through the stresses of modern life, it is wholly inadequate.[45]

A decade later the assessment has changed very little. If anything, the situation has worsened. James David Barber argues in his latest work, *The Pulse of Politics,* that "Presidents-to-be should never again be allowed to pass through the gate of an election without paying the admission of realism, talking sense to the American people about the realities he and they must fact together."[46] Ironically, as the tensions and anxieties about the future increased, so did the gap between promise and performance. The citizens, according to Barber, have become even more susceptible to grand illusions and simple answers because of their anxiety.[47] This has resulted in, first of all, a dangerous drift toward political fiction. Politics becomes "theater," "a grand game," where impression is everything. "The question of judgment is transformed into a question of appreciation — did we like the show or not?"[48] Second, as problems mount, so do expectations, many of which are simply impossible to fulfill. Candidates, however, are compelled to overpromise in order to obtain votes. Finally, the very nature of the relationship between the candidate and the public as well as the job and the job description have become distorted. The candidate becomes a star and a celebrity. He is chosen because of skills seldom related to actual job performance.

From an interactionist perspective, the difficulty of the American Presidency equally lies within the public's conception of the institution. Consequently, how can one change or alter the Presidency without first dealing with public orientations to the office. After all, politicians argue, candidates are only giving the public what they want or desire. But before potential alternatives are rendered, a careful understanding of the evolution of the "gap" is needed. Within such an understanding lies the direction of possible correction. There are three major factors which have contributed significantly to the formation of the "crisis" described above. First, previous administrations have left legacies of Presidential conduct and behavior which have been deified, contributing to the formation of legends, heroes, and expectations of spectacular behavior. This study has shown how such a process evolves and is perpetuated in society. The myth of the Presidency is strong indeed. Popular fantasy views the President as Superman. Every action and word is carefully preserved and finds their way into historical documents, textbooks, and movies. In effect, our young are taught to respect the office and to expect little less than miracles. In addition, "fame" as a personal goal is very much a part of the American dream. It is the second component of the team "rich and famous." Fame, however, has its obligations and inconveniences. Perhaps the greatest difficulty is to meet continually unrational and unrealistic expectations of the public. Even creating and sustaining an image at considerable cost of being able to "walk on water" is easier than really attempting to do so. The important point is, however, that no matter how good the intentions; a mere image always becomes enlarged and distorted. The "imperial Presidency," according to Schlesinger, began in the 1940's when Presidents asserted their control and influence in foreign affairs.[49] This same assertion began on the homefront in the 1960's with equal vigor. The result is a spiralling image of Presidential influence, salvation, and action to meet every crisis or need of the nation.

The second major factor which has contributed to the formation of the "crisis" of the Presidency is the role of mass media. The mass media, especially television, emphasizes image over substance. The media often aids in reinforcing the "myths" of Presidential persona as well as in the construction of such myths. Boorstin distinguishes between "fame" and "greatness."[50] He effectively argues that within the last century America has discovered the processes by which fame can be manufactured which heavily depends upon the mass media. Heroes have always been respected and honored in the nation. Today, however, we have replaced hero-worship with celebrity-worship. By confusing the two, according to Boorstin, the nation deprives itself of good models and comes to believe that people are great because they are famous instead of people who are famous because they are great. Heroes were distinguished by achievement gaining recognition over a long period—usually at least a generation. In contrast, laments Boorstin, the celebrity is distinguished by his image and created by the media. The celebrity is always contemporary and survives by gossip, public opinion, magazines, newspapers, and television. "Celebrities, because they are made to order, can be made to please, comfort, fascinate, and flatter us. They can be produced and displaced in rapid succession."[51] Interestingly, as Boorstin notes, a public figure used to have a private secretary to protect the individual from the public. Today, the public man must have a press secretary whose job is to keep the individual before the public at all times.

It is not simply a problem of public officials utilizing the media but also a problem of media control over the national agenda. There is little disagreement as to the media's ability to influence the issues, images, substance, and momentum of Presidential campaigns and politics. Television, of course, must bear the greatest responsibility of all the media in influencing the nature of politics. For television is the major source of political news for 65 percent of the electorate.[52] Television has an almost instant credibility and thus, indirectly, contributes to inflated public expectations. More recently, however, the role of media in influencing lives more widely acknowledged and criticized in the general public. Dependence on the media, however, is as great as ever before.

The last factor contributing to the current "crisis" of the American Presidency is the failure to appreciate how drastically the world has changed since 1932 both politically and economically. The Presidency today is certainly a new institution which had its beginnings with Franklin Roosevelt. The institution faces great challenges on three levels which reflect the new "world realities" of the 1980's. These levels encompass the elements identified by one of the most recent national conferences on the "Institutional Presidency" at Airlie House in the spring of 1974 which are serious dilemmas and difficulties facing a President today.[53] Internationally, the threat of global war continues. There has been a proliferation of the Third World powers, food shortages, population growth, and continued arms race. The United States has become vitally dependent upon other nations for oil and various imports. With increasing technology and nuclear proliferation, we can no longer compel Third World nations to respond quickly to our bidding. Domestically our nation has undergone a virtual revolution that has influenced the nature of our society. Economic forces in our nation have become unmanageable as well as uncontrollable. Our economic stability is directly linked to the economic stability of other nations. Old solutions or remedies for problems of inflation, productivity, unemployment, consumerism, and distribution are no longer effective. Finally, these problems and influences have dictated a revolution in the nature of the Presidency. The executive branch assumed more power and control in attempting to handle the "new world" crises and influences. Ironically, as the office attempted to solve more complex problems, citizen expectations increased. All of these factors, therefore, have contributed to widening the gap between largely symbolic expectations and Presidential performance. Theodore White elegantly observes:

> What was happening in the decades between 1932 and 1972 was the end of an old American myth—the myth that began with the meeting in town hall, where independent even came together and discussed the town taxes or where the town roads should run. The problems now were too complicated to be discussed in town hall; the parties were too arthritic, too stiff at the joints to flex with the changing needs of America. The press described what was happening on the broad horizon; and television translated what the press reported into emotional symbols that stimulated shock, concern, alarm, sorrow, pride. Assassinations, inaugurations, the dusty moon, the voter's conventions, the violence in the streets, the pollution of shore, stream, lake, the upheaval of the blacks, above all, the war in Vietnam—each passed into political emotion via the tube of television, and there on the tube were transformed into supercharged symbols of Good and Bad.[54]

As the gap increases so does the disillusionment of many Americans and the importance of the Presidency. What remains is a "symbol thrashing around—in search of some heartfelt connection between government and people."[55] The end result of the widening gap is to make the Presidency pure symbol with no referent and no substance. As Barber succinctly predicts:

> Take away confidence in the President's power and we the people may turn him into an entertainer, who, however seriously he may take himself need not furrow our brows with real-world calculation. ... Presidential campaigns become an extended political holiday — a trip to the nation's psychological beaches and mountains — a 'suspension of disbelief' analogous to the restful anticipation one feels just as the lights go down and the curtain goes up in the theatre. The distinction fades between actors who play candidates or Presidents (Robert Redford, Henry Fonda) and Presidents struggling to act winningly in an essentially playful politics.[56]

Footnotes

[1]Grant McConnell, *The Modern Presidency* (New York: St. Martin's Press, 1976), p. 99.

[2]Murray Edelman, *The Symbolic Uses of Politics* (Urbana: University of Illinois Press, 1977), p. 119.

[3]See Hugh Dalziel Duncan, *Communication and Social Order* (New York: Oxford University Press, 1962), pp. 93-94.

[4]For a detailed list of Presidential trivia see "Presidential Facts Your Teacher May Not Have Told You," *Friends Magazine,* Vol. 37, No. 7, July 1980, p. 10.

[5]Daniel Boorstin, *The Image* (New York: Atheneum, 1962), p. 3.

[6]Alfred de Grazia, "The Myth of the President" in *The Presidency,* Aaron Wildavsky, ed. (Boston: Little, Brown and Co., 1969), p. 50.

[7]Theodore H. White, *Breach of Faith* (New York: Atheneum Publishers, 1975), pp. 323-324.

[8]*Ibid.,* p. 324.

[9]Murray Edelman, "The Politics of Persuasion" in *Choosing the President,* James D. Barber, ed. (Englewood Cliffs: Prentice Hall, 1974), p. 160.

[10]Roger Cobb and Charles D. Elder, "Individual Orientations in the Study of Political Symbolism," *Social Science Quarterly,* June, 1972, 53, 1, p. 87.

[11]These characteristics are provided by Boorstin in discussing an "image." The "Presidency" as a symbol clearly has the same characteristics. See pp. 185-193.

[12]For an outstanding discussion of the distinction between the functioning of signs and symbols in relation to the Presidency see Michael Novak, *Choosing Our King* (New York: MacMillan, 1974), especially pp. 7-10.

[13]Edelman, *The Symbolic Uses of Politics,* p. 11.

[14]Novak, p. 8.

[15]For a discussion of specific symbols through which a President communicates to the people see Novak, p. 8.

[16]This quote by Taft appears in almost every major textbook on the Presidency. See Rossiter, *The American Presidency* (New York: 2nd Edition, Mentor Books, 1960), p. 16.

[17]*Ibid.*

[18]Thomas Cronin, *The State of the Presidency* (Boston: Little, Brown and Co., 1975), p. 239.

[19]Orrin Klapp, *Symbolic Leaders* (Chicago: Aldine Publishing, 1964), pp. 52-58.

[20]*Ibid.,* p. 58.

[21]*Ibid.,* p. 51.

[22]Novak, p. 46.

[23]Novak is good at such analysis, see Part One, pp. 3-56.

[24]*Ibid.,* p. 28.

[25]James D. Barber, "Man, Mood, and The Presidency," in *The Presidency Reappraised,* Rexford Tugwell and Thomas Cronin, eds. (New York: Praeger Publishers, 1974), p. 205.

[26]See George Reedy, *The Twilight of the Presidency* (New York: World Publishing Co., 1970).

[27]Novak, p. 20.

[28]*Ibid.,* especially pp. 3, 50-52.

[29]For a good perspective of our involvement in Vietnam and the growth of our domestic ills see Jonathan Schell, *The Time of Illusion* (New York: Vintage, 1975).

[30]Cronin, p. 7.

[31]Victor Lasky, *It Didn't Start With Watergate* (New York: Richard Marek Publications, 1977).

[32]Jimmy Carter, *Why Not the Best?* (New York: Bantam Books, 1975), p. 3.

[33]Reedy, p. xv.

[34]See Edward S. Corwin, *The President: Office and Powers* (New York: New York University Press, 1957) and Joseph Kallenbach, *The American Chief Executive* (New York: Harper & Row, 1966).

[35]See Aaron Wildavsky, *The Presidency* (Boston: Little, Brown, and Co., 1969). Also useful is "The Institutionalized Presidency," *Law and Contemporary Problems* (Duke University Law School), Vol. xxv, No. 3, Summer 1970.

[36]See David Truman, *The Governmental Process* (New York: Alfred A. Knopf, 1955) and Stanley Rothman, "Systematic Political Theory: Observations on the Group Approach," *A.P.S.R.,* 54 March, 1960).

[37]See G. Parry, *Political Elites* (New York: Pareger, 1969); C. Wright Mills, *The Power Elite* (New York: Oxford University Press, 1956); and G.W. Domhoff, *Who Rules America?* (Englewood Cliffs: Prentice Hall, 1967).

[38]See Edwin C. Hargrove, *Presidential Leadership: Personality and Political Style* (New York: MacMillan Co., 1966); Harold Lasswell, *Psychopathology and Politics* (Chicago: University of Chicago Press, 1930); and James Barber, *The Presidential Character* (Englewood Cliffs: Prentice Hall, 1972).

[39]See Richard C. Snyder, et al., *Foreign Policy Decision-Making* (New York: Free Press, 1962); Randall Ripley, et al., *Structure, Environment and Political Action: Exploring a Model of Policy-Making* (Beverly Hills: Sage Publications, 1973); David Braybrooke and Charles Lindbloom, *A Strategy of Decision* (New York: Free Press, 1963); David Easton, *A System Analysis of Political Life* (New York: Wiley and Sons, 1965); Charles Lindbloom, *The Policy-Making Process* (Englewood Cliffs: Prentice-Hall, 1968).

[40]Rossiter, p. 228.

[41]*Ibid.,* p. 237.
[42]Reedy, p. 182.
[43]Cronin, p. 5.
[44]*Ibid.,* p. 238.
[45]Reedy, p. xvii.
[46]James D. Barber, *The Pulse of Politics* (New York: Norton, 1980), p. 316.
[47]*Ibid.,* p. 316.
[48]*Ibid.,* p. 320.
[49]Arthur M. Schlesinger, *The Imperial Presidency* (Boston: Houghton Mifflin, 1973), p. 212.
[50]See Boorstin, especially pp. 47-74.
[51]*Ibid.,* p. 74.
[52]The League of Women Voters, *Choosing the President,* 1976, p. 63.
[53]For a complete report of the Conference see Ernest S. Griffith, *The American Presidency* (New York: New York University Press, 1976).
[54]White, p. 47.
[55]Barber, "Man, Mood, and the Presidency," p. 214.
[56]Barber, *The Presidential Character,* p. v.

Chapter 6

The Future of the Presidency

It is usually at this point in studies of the Presidency where one is supposed to offer concrete suggestions for reform. To offer solutions of action has become traditional if not obligatory. Yet, I refuse to fall totally for the "trap." Social analyses should not always be compelled to adopt the format of a market research report or an engineer's memorandum in order to merit respect or attention. The processes of diagnosis and prescription are separate steps, each requiring careful preparation and analysis. Symbolic interaction, as a perspective is descriptive not evaluative. Yet, "pure" description is nearly impossible. The major thrust of this study, however, has been to describe the levels of interaction of the public with the Presidency and its pathological consequences. This brief chapter, therefore, is not an attempt to summarize or analyze all the various proposals for reform of the Presidency. There already exists a large body of academic literature on the subject. However, implicit in Chapter 5 is the notion of alarm and thus speculation of a remedy. If the foregoing analysis is correct, there is a corresponding view or orientation to the Presidency that should be adopted.

Most of the solutions or reforms for the Presidency are based upon political, programmatic, or governmental factors. Intellectuals have focused rather narrowly on technical alternatives or simply given up to cynical generalities.[1] The proposals usually assume, as observed by Reedy, "that wise and effective government flows from careful study by responsible men who have access to 'all' the facts and who need only the authority and the machinery to carry out intelligently designed programs."[2] Such proposals assume that "truth" is an absolute rather than the product of interaction and shared perspectives. Identifying desirable changes is easy. However, most of the changes would demand a drastic restructuring of our institutions. Some of the proposals would indeed make the operations of the Presidency more efficient but would surely destroy the dynamic nature of the office.

To question the future of the Presidency is to question the future of the entire American political order. To "reform" the Presidency means more than changing the electoral institutions. Western peoples, argues Slater, are "mixed up" about social change.

> They tend to believe that it only takes place through conscious public policy, when in fact the changes that really matter are occurring by tiny increments every time someone buys something or builds something. They also imagine that major social changes can be achieved simply by deciding to make them.[3]

Social change is predicted on the altering of the public's cognitions, attitudes, beliefs, and values. Only after such alteration can there exist any reasonable chance of success for concrete, legislative or constitutional provisions in reforming the Presidency. Norman Thomas believed that:

> the obstacles to major change seem almost insurmountable. The diversity of American society and politics impedes the formation of majority coalitions for the passage of much substantive legislation and vastly increases the difficulty of building the sizeable coalition required to amend the constitution.[4]

Thus, at this time, realistic and humane alternatives are greatly needed.

In both the 1976 and 1980 Presidential election campaigns, the American people were asked to maintain their "faith" in the "American dream." Somehow, it was argued, a stronger, deeper, and a more encompassing belief in the "values" of America will return us once again to the quality of life that was lost. Perhaps, the "dream" has become too real. It no longer serves as motivation but rather as a "stumbling block" to confronting the current problems. As a nation, we must first disillusion ourselves. Boorstin diagnosed in 1962 that,

> What ails us most is not what we have done with America, but what we have substituted for America. We suffer primarily not from our voices or our weaknesses, but from our illusions. We are haunted not by reality, but by those images we have put in place of reality.[5]

As a nation, our greatest threat is not global war, ideology, poverty, hunger, or tyranny but simply "unreality." "The threat of nothingness is the danger of replacing American dreams by American illusions."[6] Our news, heroes, and commodities of life are all products of illusions. Nothing our nation produces, from vegematics" to "Cadillacs" are less than the "greatest," "best," or "most fantastic." Our illusions have, over time, become so vivid, persuasive, and "real" that we thrive in them.

In terms of the Presidency, the central question becomes how to continue to cultivate an active, democratic citizenry with highly inflated visions of Presidential grandeur, greatness, and salvation? Historically, there has been more consensus than disagreement about the nature of the American Presidency. Since the New Deal, the Presidency has been presented as an office of hope, direction, and moral vigor. Consequently, textbook writers and journalists have exaggerated and oversimplified the capabilities of the modern Presidency. As status and privilege begins to feed upon itself, the occupant desires "rewards" not because of the office but because of his mere existence.[7] Reedy argued in 1970 that "no one in the modern world expects a queen or a king to actually run a government.... It is far too comfortable, far too insulated from the harsh realities, to harden a man against the exigencies of statecraft."[8] The yearning for a "king" can only result in disappointment as well as severely damage a healthy democracy. For such an image of the Presidency, as already argued, affects the quality of the relationship between the office and the public. Distorted public perceptions and expectations lead to distorted Presidential behavior. As the gap widens between perceptions and "reality," between expectations and performance, there exists a real danger to American democracy. The nation cannot depend upon Congress to limit the Presidency until the popular mystique of the office is confronted. As Cronin correctly argues, "if a President is forced to respond to all the major issues of the day, he doubtless will be forced to respond mainly on the plane of symbolic and superficial politics."[9] Thus, the President's symbolic power over "reality" is the crucial issue of concern in any notion of reform. In short, no longer can the social reality of the United States be left to the definition of one man.[10] The role of fantasy and illusion further removes us from useful interaction in attempting to confront our national concerns. Philip Slater poignantly recognizes the danger of our continual reliance upon myth to confront harsh decisions. "We are born into intimate mutual-feedback relationships with our environments, both human and non-human. Commitments to fantasy break this circuit. Signals are ignored, and behavior becomes mechanical, insensitive."[11]

Of course, discovering our illusions will not solve the problems of the world. It is, however, the first step toward discovering what the real problems are. As a nation, we need to discover where our dreams end and our illusions begin. Only then can we adequately assess where we "are" and where we should "go." Such a notion is predicated on the belief that there is a need to alter the symbols of the political system before attempting to alter the outputs of the system.

But the argument presented thus far is certainly not new. Less mechanistic, structural alternatives have been suggested, especially since the Watergate affair. Some contemporary political scientists, such as Cronin, advocate "disenchantment" and moderation of the expectations of the Presidency. For too long, the public has depended upon the office and a single man to confront as well as to solve critical issues. Such a dependence has resulted in recent Presidents being less popular and serves as convenient scapegoats for the mounting pressures of today's world. Second, some have argued that there should be changes in the character of the Presidency as a symbol of benevolence and deference. To demythicize the Presidency is to alter the socialization process instilling in the public a sense of confidence, competence, and criticalness ultimately instituting a device for the immediate removal of a President lacking responsiveness and confidence of the country as well as Congress. Third, some Presidential scholars advise that the nation should always request Presidents to give their best but never require them to deliver more than the office or a single person has to give.

In calling for the demythification of the Presidency, one feels as the villain who proclaims to young children that "there really is no Santa Claus." But are we, as a nation, really "foolish" enough to believe the Presidential persona and drama or is it really a question of *wanting* to believe in the myth. Yet, where does one draw the line between fiction and "reality?" At least this study has attempted to recognize the depth of the mythic, symbolic nature of the Presidency. Consequently, the study may even contribute to a greater appreciation for the symbolic dimensions of the office. But does one dare condone or encourage an attitude of "heads in the clouds" when today there appears to be so many dangers lurking about? Has the time come when the visions are more dangerous than reassuring? I, indeed, believe so.

The call for altering citizen attitudes of the office has increased significantly in the last decade. Specifically, Reedy, Schlesinger, and Cronin have all argued for a little "healthy" skeptical disrespect and lower expectations of the Presidency.[12] They argue that such an attitude by the public will make Presidents more responsive and attuned to reality. Some have even suggested a total detachment of the symbolic function from the chief executive. The British Monarchy and Prime Minister surface as the model for encouraging the adoption of a cabinet form of government. Yet, the legislature as the principal policy advocate has a rich history founded upon the Madisonian view of the Presidency. The point is, such notions have had little impact and tend to be temporary or transitory. The reason for such failure has been the lack of acknowledgment or full appreciation for the special relationship between the symbolic Presidency and the American people. Such proposals, in the past, according to Buchanan, do not "reflect appreciation for the fact that citizens need an anthropomorphic symbol of government, and that they will—in the long run—tend to idealize that human symbol."[13]

In addition, I am not so sure that encouraging disrespect or skepticism is really the proper word. For it is comparable to giving the reigns of power and responsibility to a subordinate and then carefully monitoring and following every step—anticipating failure or the arising of problems. Would it not be better to give the reigns of control knowing the full limitations of the individual and job description? Being "realistic" is not the same as being "paranoid" or "overprotective."

Early in the Carter Presidency, observers were noting an apparent change of public attitudes toward the office. Jimmy Carter responded by de-emphasizing the symbolic, royal dimensions of the office. But by mid-term the public wanted to see the President in a suit and not jeans; hear "Hail to the Chief" and not "Dixie"; to receive a formal presentation of the state of the union and not an informal discussion over coffee.

What is really being advocated by some scholars is that Americans must, first of all, become fair and realistic. The nation must realize that history has created an institution of exaggerated expectations of performance. Realism is needed in recognizing the limits of the office. The nation has overloaded the institution. Although more realistic expectations alone will not cure the office or the ills of the nation, they will relieve some of the burden, thus enabling a President to attack major problems more realistically. Being fair means recognizing that large scale problems require large scale solutions demanding patience, cooperation, and planning—not simplistic, ad hoc, campaign promises to meet visions of immediate salvation. That luxury is no longer (if it ever was) available.

Finally, civic responsibility and initiative should once again become a keystone of social life. Waiting for others to solve critical problems is at best a risky alternative. As John Kennedy proclaimed in concluding his inaugural address, "...let us go forth to lead the land we love, asking His blessing and His help, but knowing that here on earth God's work must truly be our own."[14] Many Presidential observers, historians, and scholars have characterized the relationship of the Presidency and the American people as one of a parent to child relationship. Yet, as every parent knows and child finds out, a time comes when a child must become responsible, assertive in creating a life of his own. The trick, of course, is when—at what age should a child "grow up?" If too early, a child may become injured, make major mistakes, and get into serious trouble. If too late, however, the child will always be dependent, lacking the ability of sound judgment and critical thinking. Perhaps our forefathers left such a vague constitution believing that the American people are an independent lot not requiring detailed, parental instructions on the fabric of society. Have we become so old, after two hundred years, to be senile, to be reverting back to childhood dependencies?

These general suggestions sound very nice. But, "Are they practicable?" I suspect that they are not. However, any solution or proposal for changing the Presidency is doomed to failure or at least to harsh skepticism because of the nature of interaction and the symbolic function of the office. Americans, because of the increased importance of mass media, have greater access to the Presidency. Perhaps in increasing the "quantity" of interaction of the public with the office the "quality" of the interaction has decreased. No longer is it necessary or even possible for a candidate or President to confront many Americans face to face. Even when they do, the event is usually controlled to ensure proper media coverage. There is little hope, however, that more contact with Presidents will occur. The campaign season, for many, is already too long and the demands of the "job" forces Presidents to remain "home" rather than to travel around the country. In fact, Americans tend to prefer that their Presidents remain at the helm rather than to "enjoy" travel.

The greatest difficulty, however, in attempting to change the office is grounded in its fundamentally symbolic nature. As a symbol, the Presidency has "grown" such that no man can fulfill its requirements. Yet, for man, there will always be symbols. Every society will have myths. Attempts to redefine the symbol or the Presidency is possible, but the task would be long and difficult. Since the 1960's, Black America symbolically redefined its history and personage in more positive terms. The key, of course, is to *believe* in the "symbols" and receive, through interaction, positive response to the new definitions.

The President of the United States is not like the Chairman of Mobil Oil. If he were, job efficiency could more easily be instituted by structural changes. Rather, the President is symbolic. The office "represents" more than the elements identified in its job description. For this reason, the Presidency is difficult to change and continues to serve, especially in difficult times, as a source of American pride reflecting the nation's "values." The only confident and reassuring conclusion to offer is that the Presidency *is* whatever Americans choose to make it.

Footnotes

[1] James D. Barber, *The Pulse of Politics* (New York: Norton, 1980), see his discussion, p. 322.
[2] George Reedy, *The Twilight of the Presidency* (New York: The World Publishing Co., 1970), p. 138.
[3] Philip Slater, *Earthwalk* (New York: Anchor Books, 1974), p. 137.

[4]Norman C. Thomas, "Reforming the Presidency" in *The Presidency Reappraised,* Thomas Cronin and Rexford Tugwell, eds. (Praeger Publishers, 1977), p. 341.

[5]Daniel Boorstin, *The Image* (New York: Atheneum, 1962), p. 6.

[6]*Ibid.,* p. 240.

[7]See Reedy for effects of Presidential "environment" upon individual.

[8]*Ibid.,* p. 165.

[9]Thomas Cronin, *The State of the Presidency* (Boston: Little, Brown, and Co., 1975), p. 240.

[10]See Michael Novak, *Choosing Our King* (New York: MacMillan Publishing Co., 1974), p. 259.

[11]Slater, p. 211.

[12]See Reedy, Cronin, and Arthur Schlesinger, *The Imperial Presidency* (Boston: Houghton Mifflin Co., 1973).

[13]Bruce Buchanan, *The Presidential Experience* (Englewood Cliffs: Prentice Hall, 1978), p. 71.

[14]John F. Kennedy, "Inaugural Address" in *Contemporary American Speeches,* Linkugel et al, (Iowa: Kendall/Hunt Publishing Co., 1978), p. 370.

Bibliography

Allison, Graham. *Essence of Decision.* Boston: Little, Brown and Co., 1971.

Almond, G. and J. Coleman. *The Politics of the Developing Areas.* Princeton: University Press, 1960.

Almond, Gabriel and Sidney Verba. *The Civic Culture.* Princeton: Princeton University Press, 1963.

Bachrach, Peter. *The Theory of Democratic Elitism.* Boston: Little, Brown, and Co., 1967.

Barber, James. *The Presidential Character.* Englewood Cliffs: Prentice Hall, 1972.

Barber, James. *Choosing the President.* New Jersey: Prentice Hall, 1974.

Barber, James. "Man, Mood, and The Presidency." *The Presidency Reappraised.* Ed. Rexford Tugwell and Thomas Cronin, New York. Praeger Publishers, 1974, 205-216.

Barber, James. *The Pulse of Politics.* New York: Norton, 1980.

Becker, Lee, et al. "The Development of Political Cognitions." *Political Communication: Issues and Strategies for Research.* Eds. Steven Chaffee et al. Beverly Hills: Sage Publications, 1975, 21-64.

Bentley, Arthur. *The Process of Government.* Cambridge: The Belknap Press, 1967.

Berelson, Bernard et al. *Voting.* Chicago: The University of Chicago Press, 1954.

Bernstein, Carl and Bob Woodward. *All the President's Men.* New York: Simon and Schuster, 1974.

Bishop, Jim. *A Day in the Life of President Johnson.* New York: Random House, 1967.

Blumer, Herbert. *Symbolic Interactionism: Perspective and Method.* Englewood Cliffs: Prentice Hall, 1969.

Blumer, Herbert. "Society as Symbolic Interaction." *Symbolic Interaction: A Reader in Social Psychology.* Ed. Jerome Manis and Bernard Meltzer. Boston: Allyn and Bacon, 1978, 97-103.

Boorstin, Daniel. *The Image.* New York: Atheneum, 1962.

Boulding, Kenneth. *The Image: Knowledge in Life and Society.* Ann Arbor: University of Michigan Press, 1961.

Braybrooke, David and Charles Lindbloom. *A Strategy of Decision.* New York: Free Press, 1963.

Brinkley, Wilfred. *The Man in the White House. His Powers and Duties.* Baltimore: The Johns Hopkins Press, 1958.

Browlow, Louis. "What We Expect the President to Do." *The Presidency.* Ed. Aaron Wildavsky. Boston: Little, Brown and Co., 1969, 35-43.

Buchanan, Bruce. *The Presidential Experience.* Englewood Cliffs: Prentice Hall, 1978.

Burke, Kenneth. *Language As Symbolic Action.* Berkeley: University of California Press, 1966.

Burke, Kenneth. "Dramatism." *International Encyclopedia of the Social Sciences.* New York, 1968, 445-452.

Burke, Kenneth. *Grammar of Motives.* Berkeley: University of California Press, 1969.

Burke, Kenneth. "Dramatism." *Communication Concepts and Perspectives.* Ed. Lee Thayer. New Jersey: Hayden Book Co.

Burns, James McGregor. *Presidential Government: The Crucible of Leadership.* Boston: Houghton Mifflin Co., 1965.

Campbell, Angus et al. *The American Voter.* New York: John Wiley and Sons, 1960.

Campbell Bruce. *The American Electorate.* New York: Holt, Rinehart, and Winston, 1979.

Carter, Jimmy. *Why Not the Best?* New York: A Bantam Book, 1975.

Charon, Joel. *Symbolic Interactionism: An Introduction, An Interpretation, An Integration.* Englewood Cliffs: Prentice Hall, 1979.

Cobb, Roger and Charles D. Elder. "Individual Orientations in the Study of Political Symbolism." *Social Science Quarterly,* 53, 1 (June 1972), 79-90.

Collins, Randall. "Interpretive Social Psychology." *Symbolic Interaction: A Reader in Social Psychology.* Ed. Jerome Manis and Bernard Meltzer. Boston: Allyn and Bacon, 1978, 397-400.

Connolly, William. *The Bias of Pluralism.* New York: Atherton Press, 1969.

Cooper, Chester. *The Last Crusade: America in Vietnam.* New York: Dodd, Mead, 1970.

Corwin, Edward. *The President: Office and Powers.* 3rd Ed. New York: New York University Press, 1948.

Cronin, Thomas. "The Presidency Public Relations Script." *The Presidency Reappraised.* Eds. Rexford Tugwell and Thomas Cronin. New York: Praeger Publishers, 1974, 168-187.

Cronin, Thomas. *The State of the Presidency.* Boston: Little, Brown, and Co., 1975.

Cronin, Thomas. "The Presidency and Its Paradoxes." *The Presidency Reappraised: Second Edition.* Eds. Thomas Cronin and Rexford Tugwell. New York: Praeger Publishers, 1977, 69-85.

Dawson, R.E. and K. Prewith. *Political Socialization.* Boston: Little, Brown, and Co., 1969.

de Grazia, Alfred. "The Myth of the President." *The Presidency.* Ed. Aaron Wildavsky. Boston: Little, Brown, and Co., 1969, 49-73.

Dennis, J. *Socialization to Politics: A Reader.* New York: Wiley, 1973.

Domhoff, G.W. *Who Rules America?* Englewood Cliffs: Prentice Hall, 1967.

Duncan Hugh. *Communication and Social Order.* New York: Oxford University Press, 1962.

Duncan, Hugh. *Symbols in Society.* New York: Oxford University Press, 1968.

Easton, David and Robert Hess. "The Child's Political World." *Midwest Journal of Political Science,* 3 (August 1962), 229-246.

Easton, David. *The Political System.* New York: Alfred Knopf, 1953.

Easton, David. *A Systems Analysis of Political Life.* New York: Wiley, 1965.

Edelman, Murray. *The Symbolic Uses of Politics.* Urbana: University of Illinois Press, 1964.

Edelman, Murray. *Politics As Symbolic Action.* Chicago: Markham Publishing Co., 1971.

Edelman, Murray. "The Politics of Persuasion." *Choosing the President.* Ed. James D. Barber. Englewood Cliffs: Prentice Hall, 1974, 149-174.

Eisenhower, Dwight D. "Some Thoughts on the Presidency." *The Power of the Presidency.* Ed. Robert Hirschfield. Chicago: Aldine Publishing Co., 2nd Ed., 1973, 118-123.

Every Four Years: A Study of the Presidency. Public Broadcasting Service, 1980.

Faules, Don and Dennis Alexander. *Communication and Social Behavior: A Symbolic Interaction Perspective.* Mass.: Addison-Wesley Publishing, 1978.

Fisher, Walter. "Rhetorical Fiction and the Presidency." *Quarterly Journal of Speech.* 66, 2 (April 1980), 119-126.

Flanigan, William. *Political Behavior of the American Electorate.* Boston: Allyn and Bacon, 1968.

Ford, Gerald. *A Time to Heal.* New York: Harper and Row, 1979.

Gerth, Hans and C. Wright Mills. "Institutions and Persons." *Symbolic Interaction: A Reader in Social Psychology.* Ed. Jerome Manis and Bernard Meltzer. Boston: Allyn and Bacon, 1978, 116-119.

Graber, Doris. "Personal Qualities in Presidential Images: The Contribution of the Press." *Midwest Journal of Political Science,* 16 (February 1972), 46-76.

Greenstein, Fred. "Popular Images of the President." *The Presidency.* Ed. Aaron Wildavsky. Boston: Little, Brown and Co., 1969, 287-295.

Greenstein, Fred. "What the President Means to Americans." *Choosing the President.* Ed. James D. Barber. Englewood Cliffs: Prentice Hall, 1974, 121-147.

Griffith, Ernest. *The American Presidency.* New York: New York University Press, 1976.

Haight, David and Larry Johnston. *The President: Roles and Powers.* Chicago: Rand McNally, 1965.

Haldeman, H.R. *The Ends of Power.* New York: Times Books, 1978.

Hale, Myron. "Presidential Influence, Authority, and Power and Economic Policy" to be published in a *Festschrift* in honor of Francis D. Wormuth. The selection is also contained in the author's forthcoming book on *The President and the Policy Process.*

Hale, Myron. *The President and the Policy Process.* To be published.

Hall, Peter. "A Symbolic Interactionist Analysis of Politics." *Sociological Inquiry,* 42, (1972), 3-4, 35-73.

Hargrove, Edwin. *Presidential Leadership: Personality and Political Style.* New York: MacMillan, 1966.

Hess, Stephen. *The Presidential Campaign.* Washington: The Brookings Institute, 1974.

Hughes, Emmet. *The Living Presidency.* New York: Penguin Books, 1973.

Hyman, Sidney. "What is the President's True Role?" *The President: Roles and Powers.* Ed. David Haight and Larry Johnston. Chicago: Rand McNally, 1965, 31-38.

James, William. "The Social Self." *Social Psychology Through Symbolic Interaction.* Ed. Gregory Stone and Harvey Farberman. Mass.: Ginn-Blaisdell, 1970, 373-376.

Johnson, Lyndon. *The Vantage Point.* New York: Holt, Rinehart, and Winston, 1971.

Kallenbach, Joseph. *The American Chief Executive.* New York: Harper and Row, 1966.

Kaplan, Morton. *Macropolitics.* Chicago: Aldine Publishing, 1969.

Kariel, Henry. *The Promise of Politics.* Englewood Cliffs: Prentice Hall, 1966.

Kennedy, John F. "Inaugural Address." *Contemporary American Speeches.* Ed. Linkugel. Iowa: Kendall/Hunt Publishing Co., 1978, 366-369.

Klapp, Orin. *Symbolic Leaders.* Chicago: Aldine Publishing, 1964.

Koenig, Louis. *The Chief Executive.* New York: Harcourt, Brace and World, 1964.

Kotter, John. *Power in Management.* New York: AMACOM, 1979.

Kraus, S. "Mass Communication and Political Socialization: Reassessment of Two Decades of Research." *Quarterly Journal of Speech,* 59 (December), 390-400.

Lasky, Victor. *It Didn't Start With Watergate.* New York: Richard Marek Publications, 1977.

Lasswell, Harold. *Psychopathology and Politics.* Chicago: University of Chicago Press, 1930.

Lasswell, Harold. *The Decision Process.* College Park: University of Maryland, 1956.

Lasswell, Harold. *Politics: Who Gets What, When, How.* Cleveland: The World Publishing Co., 1958.

Lauer, Robert and Warren Handel. *Social Psychology: The Theory and Application of Symbolic Interaction.* Boston: Houghton Mifflin, 1977.

Lindbloom, Charles. *A Strategy of Decision.* New York: Free Press, 1963.

Lindbloom, Charles. *The Policy-Making Process.* Englewood Cliffs: Prentice Hall, 1968.

Lindesmith, Alfred et al. *Social Psychology.* Illinois: Dryden Press, 1975.

London, Perry. *Behavior Control.* New York: Meridian Books, 1977.

Long, Norton. "The Political Act as an Act of Will." *The Political Vocation.* Ed. Paul Tillett. New York: Basic Books, Inc., 1965, 178-182.

Machiavelli, Niccolo. *The Prince.* Translator Mark Musca. New York: St. Martin's Press, 1964,

McConnell, Grant. *The Modern Presidency.* New York: St. Martin's Press, 1976.

McDonald, Lee. "Myth, Politics, and Political Science." *The Western Political Quarterly.* 22 (1969), 141-150.

McGinnis, Joe. *The Selling of the President 1968.* New York: Trident Press, 1969.

McGuire, W.J. "The Nature of Attitudes and Attitude Change." *The Handbook of Social Psychology.* Eds. Lindzey and E. Aronson, Vol. 3, Mass: Addison-Wesley, 1969, 136-314.

Mead, George H. *Mind, Self, and Society.* Chicago: University of Chicago Press, 1972.

Meltzer, Bernard and John Petras. "The Chicago and Iowa Schools of Symbolic Interactionism." *Human Nature and Collective Behavior.* Ed. Tamotsu Shibutani. Englewood Cliffs: Prentice Hall, 1970, 6-14.

Meltzer, Bernard, et al. "Varieties of Symbolic Interactionism." *Symbolic Interaction: A Reader in Social Psychology.* Ed. Jerome Manis and Bernard Meltzer. Boston: Allyn and Bacon, 1978, 41-56.

Mills, C. Wright. *The Power Elite.* New York: Oxford University Press, 1956.

Miyamoto, Frank. "Self, Motivation, and Symbolic Interactionist Theory." *Human Nature and Collective Behavior.* Ed. Tamotsu Shibutani. Englewood Cliffs: Prentice Hall, 1970, 271-285.

Mosca, Gaetano. *The Ruling Class.* New York: McGraw Hill, 1939.

Mueller, Claus. *The Politics of Communication.* New York: Oxford University Press, 1973.

Mullen, William. *Presidential Power and Politics.* New York: St. Martin's Press, 1976.

Neustadt, Richard. *Presidential Power.* New York: John Wiley and Sons, 1960.

Nimmo, Dan. *The Political Persuaders.* Englewood Cliffs: Prentice Hall, 1970.

Nimmo, Dan. *Political Communication and Public Opinion in America.* California: Goodyear Publishing Co., 1978.

Nixon, Richard. *The Memoirs of Richard Nixon.* New York: Grosset and Dunlop, 1978.

Norton, Thomas. *The Constitution of the United States: Its Sources and Its Application.* New York: Committee for Constitutional Government, 1965.

Novak, Michael. *Choosing Our King.* New York: MacMillan Publishing Co., 1974.

Olsen, Marvin. *The Process of Social Organization.* New York: Holt, Rinehart, and Winston, 1968.

Orman, John. *Presidential Secrecy and Deception: Beyond the Power to Persuade.* Connecticut: Greenwood Press, 1980.

Overington, Michael. "Kenneth Burke and the Method of Dramatism." *Theory and Society.* Vol. 4, No. 1 (Spring 1977), 129-156.

Parry, G. *Political Elites.* New York: Praeger, 1969.

Pious, Richard. *The American Presidency.* New York: Basic Books, 1979.

Polsby, Nelson and Aaron Wildavsky. *Presidential Elections.* New York: Charles Scribner's Sons, 1971.

Pomper, Gerald. *Voter's Choice.* New York: Harper and Row, 1975.

Pranger, Robert. *Action, Symbolism, and Action.* Nashville: Vanderbilt University Press, 1968.

"Presidential Facts Your Teacher May Not Have Told You." *Friends Magazine,* Vol. 37, No. 7 (July 1980), 10-11.

Reedy, George. *The Twilight of the Presidency.* New York: World Publishing Co., 1970.

Reedy, George. "On the Isolation of Presidents." *The Presidency Reappraised: Second Edition.* Eds. Thomas Cronin and Rexford Tugwell. New York: Praeger Publishers, 1977, 190-198.

Ripley, Randall et al. *Structure, Environment and Political Action: Exploring a Model of Policy-Making.* Beverly Hills: Sage Publications, 1973.

Rose, Richard. *People in Politics: Observations Across the Atlantic.* New York: Basic Books, 1965.

Rossiter, Clinton. *The American Presidency.* New York: Mentor Books, 1962.

Rothman, Stanley. "Systematic Political Theory: Observations on the Group Approach." *A.P.S.R.* 54 (March 1960), 15-33.

Schandler, H. *The Unmaking of a President: LBJ and Vietnam.* Princeton: Princeton University Press, 1977.

Schell, Jonathan. *The Time of Illusion.* New York: Vintage, 1975.

Schlesinger, Arthur. *A Thousand Days.* Conn.: A Fawcett Premier Book, 1965.

Schlesinger, Arthur. *The Imperial Presidency.* Boston: Houghton Mifflin Co., 1973.

Sears, D.O. "Political Behavior." *The Handbook of Social Psychology.* Eds. Lindzey and E. Aronson. Mass.: Addison-Wesley, 1969, 315-388.

Seligman, Lester and Michael Baer. "Expectations of Presidential Leadership in Decision-Making." *The Presidency.* Ed. Aaron Wildavsky. Boston: Little, Brown, and Co., 1969, 18-34.

Sereno, Renzo. *The Rulers.* New York: Frederick Praeger, 1962.

Sidey, Hugh. "Shadow Dancing with the World." *Time.* December 31, 1979, 20.

Sidey, Hugh. "The Presidency: Change in the Set of the Jaw." *Time,* November 12, 1979, 26.

Sigel, R. "Political Socialization: Its Role in the Political Process." *Annals of the American Academy of Political and Social Science,* 361 (September 1965).

Slater, Philip. *Earthwalk.* New York: Anchor Books, 1974.

Snyder, Richard et al. *Foreign Policy Decision-Making.* New York: Free Press, 1962.

Thach, Charles C. *The Creation of the Presidency.* Baltimore: The Johns Hopkins Press, 1969.

"The Institutionalized Presidency." *Law and Contemporary Problems.* Duke University Law School. Vol. XXV. No. 3 (Summer 1970).

Thomas, Norman. "Reforming the Presidency." *The Presidency Reappraised: Second Edition.* Eds. Thomas Cronin and Rexford Tugwell. New York: Praeger Publishers, 1977, 321-344.

Truman, David. *The Governmental Process.* New York: Alfred A. Knopf, 1951.

Truman, Harry. *Memoirs: Years of Decisions,* Vol. 1. New York: Doubleday, 1955.

Tullock, Gordon. *The Politics of Bureaucracy.* Washington: Public Affairs Press, 1965.

Turner, Jonathan. "Symbolic Interactionism and Social Organization." *Symbolic Interaction: A Reader in Social Psychology.* Ed. Jerome Manis and Bernard Meltzer. Boston: Allyn and Bacon, 1978, 400-402.

Turner, Robert. *I'll Never Lie To You: Jimmy Carter in His Own Words.* New York: Ballantine Books, 1976.

von Hoffman, Nicholas. *Make-Believe Presidents: Illusions of Power from McKinley to Carter.* New York: Pantheon Books, 1978.

Weinstein, Michael. *Philosophy, Theory, and Method in Contemporary Political Thought.* Glenview: Scott, Foresman, and Co., 1971.

White, Theodore. *The Making of the President 1960.* New York: Atheneum Publishers, 1961.

White, Theodore. *Breach of Faith.* New York: Atheneum Publishers, 1975.

Wiseman, H. *Political Systems.* New York: Frederick Praeger, 1967.

Wooten, James. *Dasher: The Roots and Rising of Jimmy Carter.* New York: Warner Books, 1978.

Index